A
STRAIGHTFORWARD GUIDE
TO
WRITING ROMANTIC FICTION

KATE WALKER

Straightforward Publishing
Brighton BN2 4EG

© Cathy Wade 2007

British cataloguing in publication data. A catalogue record of this
publication is available in the British Library.

ISBN 1 84716 016 6
ISBN 13: 9781847160164

Printed by Biddles Ltd Kings Lynn Norfolk

Cover design by Bookworks Islington

CONTENTS

A STRAIGHTFORWARD GUIDE TO WRITING ROMANTIC FICTION

Introduction

This revised addition of Writing Romantic Fiction is intended to provide information and advice for anyone who wants to learn how to write Romantic fiction. It gives a short introduction to all the essential skills needed to succeed, from initial research to the final submission of the typescript.

The book covers the following:

-Creating sympathetic heroines

-Portraying irresistible heroes

-Writing effective dialogue

-Inventing readable plots

-Working from different viewpoints

-Putting in sensual scenes

-Beginnings and endings

-Finding the right setting

-Submitting your typescript

Additional materials include key points at the end of each chapter and a romance writer's resource and research checklist. There is also a selected booklist of further reading and details of relevant writer's associations.

1

BEFORE YOU BEGIN

Why write romance?

Romantic fiction is one of the best selling forms of fiction throughout the world. It is read and enjoyed by millions of women of all ages and from all backgrounds in every country. Around between 40 or 50 per cent of all paperback novels sold in bookshops around the world are romantic fiction, and almost 12 per cent of books borrowed from public libraries are romantic novels.

The authors of such books can become household names like Catherine Cookson and Barbara Taylor Bradford and they have fans who will buy each new book as soon as it appears. In America there are magazines and bookshops devoted specifically to romantic fiction. Unlike other genres whose popularity fluctuates up and down, the popularity of romances stays consistently high.

What is a romance?

A romance is basically a novel about human relationships. It is about people and how they interact together. Usually, this means the relationships between men and women, the traditional 'love story'. Essentially, it tells of the development of a relationship between a hero and heroine. Although there may be other elements, the focus is an intense concern with the focal relationship. This plot can be summarised as 'Boy meets girl. They fall in love. There are problems that keep them apart. These problems are resolved and there is a happy ending.'

These are the bare bones of the romance novel. But not all such novels are exactly alike. Depending on the market it is aimed for, a romance can have elements of fantasy, suspense, history or medicine. So before you start, you need to decide exactly what sort of romance you want to write.

What do romance readers want?

Escapism is the word most often used to describe romantic fiction. But readers don't simply want to be distracted from everyday, humdrum reality; they also want an emotional experience, the more intense the better. They want to feel that dreams can come true, that romantic love does exist. They want to experience, through the heroine, the excitement of being swept off their feet.

But at the same time they don't want the story to be such a fantasy that they can't possibly believe in any of it or have characters who are so fantastic that they are almost laughable. It doesn't have to be set on some exotic island or in an atmosphere of glamour and glitz. Readers want heroines they can identify with and heroes who excite and intrigue them. They want rounded characters who are believable, with understandable flaws and a touch of vulnerability that they can relate to.

Why do *you* want to write a romance?

Many people believe that writing romantic fiction is the quick route to fame and fortune. They hear stories of novels on the best-seller lists, huge advances, see writer's pictures in magazines, and believe that this will happen to them. They are convinced that because the books are easy to read, they are also easy to write and they will soon make a lot of money.

Some romance writers do make it big and earn that fortune, but there are plenty of others who don't. Most make a reasonable living from their writing, after a time. But it takes a while to build up a reputation and gain readers. There is a lot of competition for very few openings with publishers. For example, Harlequin Mills & Boon receive over 5,000 manuscripts a year and they reject around 90% of them.

If your only reasons for writing romantic fiction are the thought of the fame and the money you will earn then it will show in your work and the book will not be the satisfying experience readers expect. But it you love what you do and write for personal fulfilment, because you have a story you just have to tell, you are much more likely to be successful.

Telling a special kind of story

Some writers have tried to produce romances while scorning and laughing at the genre. Some have tried to write to a 'formula', believing it was simply a question of combining certain elements to produce the right effect. This approach leads to failure. The romance is special because it demands that you immerse yourself in its particular conventions and language. It is a very different, enclosed world and you have to try and live in that world, not just visit it to observe like a tourist.

In romance, everything depends on whether you can get inside your characters' skin. You can write an absolutely minimalist plot, but if your hero and heroine's thoughts and feelings are central to your writing you can still create a powerful romance. Just being able to tell a story is not enough. You have to be able to show the developing personalities of your central characters, how and why they change, and how they arrive at a point where they are emotionally able to commit themselves to a relationship.

Can you write a romance?

Before you even start to write, you should consider whether romance is really the sort of novel you should be writing. Consider these questions. The answers you give to them

10

should help you decide whether it's the form of fiction that will suit you.

1. Are you interested in people and knowing what makes them tick?
2. Do you like to read 'human interest' stories or biographies of famous people in newspapers, magazines and books?
3. Do you notice what people look like, what they're wearing, their mood, how they walk and talk?
4. Do you 'people watch' when you're in cafés etc, observing passers-by and wondering where they're going, who they might meet?
5. Do you appreciate the differences between men and women and take an interest in the problems and joys that relationship can bring?
6. Do you prefer films that show a developing relationship between characters rather than a straight action adventure or a comedy?
7. Do you enjoy the soaps and get involved with the characters and their stories?
8. Most of all, do you read and enjoy novels with a romantic element to them by choice?

Types of romance

The word Romance covers a wide range of different types of novels, and before you start to put pen to paper you should decide exactly which sort of book you want to write.

Some critics claim that all romances, particularly the short, 'category' romances such as the ones produced by Harlequin Mills & Boon, are the same, but this is not the case. Every writer has their own unique way of telling a story which gives them their individual 'voice'.

Even within a category, such as Harlequin Mills & Boon's Contemporary Romances, there are two distinct strands:

Romance where each novel tells a warm, tender love story told in the emotional way that has been accepted as the more traditional approach.

Modern which are more passionate, provocative stories. These novels are much more sensual in tone and can tackle difficult contemporary issues in sophisticated, compelling storylines.

Other types of romances that are published include:

- Historical romance where the period setting has to be accurate
- Medical romances. These are more than just 'doctor-nurse' stories. Hospital settings and any medical details included should be factually correct
- Suspense. The romantic thriller which blends a romance with a thriller plot
- The 'Aga saga' as in the novels of writers such as Joanna Trollope
- Family sagas covering generations of the same family and their joys and tragedies. These can be modern or historical.
- Gothic romance where mystery, the paranormal and romance are blended together
- Science fiction.
- Westerns
- The blockbuster – a big, glamorous novel covering a wide range of characters and settings.

What sort of romance should you write?

How can you decide which type of romantic novel is the one you are best suited to write?

The only way you can do this is to do your market research and read, read, read.

Read as many novels as you can, selecting them from as many of the different types of romances as possible and reading the work of a large variety of authors, not just one or two. Read them all with an open mind, if you approach them with cynicism and contempt you will never learn what it is about them that makes them appeal to so many readers.

Make notes about what you have read, logging your responses to each of them. Find out which ones excite you, which leave you cold. Do you prefer a short, fast-paced novel or a long, absorbing read? A modern setting or historical?

Ask yourself whether you have any knowledge or experience – in a hospital, for example, or as a police officer or living for some time in a foreign country - that would give you a particular strength in writing one type of book. Are you prepared to do the necessary research to ensure that a historical book is factually accurate?

Try out how you feel about writing each type of book by attempting short pieces of writing in the style of each one – a typical piece of description, for example, or dialogue that would fit with the characters in each form of novel. But remember that a publisher is looking for an individual spark that makes you special. They do *not* want a pale imitation of an already well-established author.

When you consider your responses to these suggestions you should be able to make a well-judged selection of the type of book you should try writing.

Now read the KEY POINTS from Chapter One.

KEY POINTS
BEFORE YOU BEGIN

- Think carefully about why you want to write a romance. If it is just a commercial exercise, you are unlikely to succeed.

- Read as many books of romantic fiction in as many different styles as you can to find out which type you enjoy most.

- Note the elements that make up each particular type of story and your own responses to them to help you decide which one you want to write.

- Try out some typical passages from each sort of book and try to give them your own individual 'voice'.

2

CREATING CHARACTERS – THE HEROINE

Having decided what sort of romance you want to write, you are now ready to start considering specific details. The first one to concentrate on is the character of your heroine.

Why is the heroine so important?

As the majority of readers of romantic fiction are women, the character of the heroine is central to their enjoyment of the novel. She is the gateway through which the reader enters the story. For the duration of the novel, the reader *becomes* the heroine and sees everything through her eyes, knowing her thoughts, sympathising with her feelings and even making the same mistakes of judgement she makes.

So your novel can stand or fall on the character of your heroine. If the reader finds her unsympathetic, unbelievable or downright incomprehensible, then a great deal of the interest and enjoyment in the book can be lost and she is unlikely to want to finish the story. But a sympathetic, interesting heroine, one the reader cares about, will hold their attention to the very last page.

Getting rid of some myths

Many people believe that there is a stereotype of a heroine, that she must be young, defenceless, inexperienced, virginal, and of course impossibly beautiful. She is the heroine of the old-fashioned fairy story, Cinderella, Snow White, or Sleeping Beauty, just waiting for her prince to come and rescue her from her life of drudgery or kiss her and awaken her from her deep sleep.

Such heroines may have been popular in the past, but can you really see them working today? Modern readers want to have novels about women like themselves, women who live in the twenty-first century with all the benefits and problems that modern living brings. They want heroines whose lifestyles reflect their own, from every type of background, with careers, relationships, families, children, money problems, the lot.

And heroines are no longer always young and innocent. Many novels feature older, mature women, who have lived full lives and have had other relationships in the past. Love and romance are not exclusive to the young, but belong to the young at heart who can be any age from nineteen to ninety.

Finally, heroines do not just sit around waiting for 'Mr Right' to sweep them off their feet. They have full lives, demanding jobs and are certainly not living in limbo without a man. It's no longer the case of a woman *needing* a man to make her life worth living, but her *wanting* a partner who can share its ups and downs, enhance its pleasures and help through the difficult times.

Creating a believable heroine

Your choice of the type of novel you want to write will affect the way you create your heroine and the sort of character she is. A novel set during the Civil War would need a very different kind of heroine to one set in the glamorous, modern world of television production or international banking. An independent, unconventional character then would get a very different reaction to the one a more modern heroine would receive.

So you have to consider the world you are going to put your heroine into before you start to create a rounded, believable character.

Names

Obviously, your heroine must have a name, but before you christen her you should consider the following points:

- How does a person's name affect your impression of them or their character, especially before you even meet them? Buy or borrow a dictionary of first names and browse through it, reading the meanings given for each one, and think about how you react to particular names. How might a Leonora be different from a Mavis? Would you expect Tallulah to be a drama queen, or see Dorothy as a quiet little mouse?

- What about nicknames? They can tell you something about both the person who is given them and the one who creates the name. One woman could be christened Elizabeth, but be Liz, Lizzie, Beth, Liza, Libby or Betty to a variety of friends or relations who would all clearly see her slightly differently.

- Remember what historical period or what country you are writing about and name your heroine in a way that is appropriate. A Regency heroine is not going to be called Kylie, and a Russian princess is unlikely to be named Madge.

- Make sure that her name combines well with her surname –and that of the hero, because of course she will end up married to him. If Heidi Brown married Mr High, she would end up as Heidi High!

- Finally, think about who gave your heroine her name – usually her parents – and why. For example, if her parents longed for a son but got a daughter instead, they might give her a masculine sounding name such as Charlie or Robyn. How would this affect her as she was growing up? It could also lead to an interesting mix-up if the hero was expecting a man by that name.

Appearance

Readers can't identify with your heroine unless they have a very clear idea of what she looks like. You need to have a very clear picture of your heroine's physical appearance in your mind so that you can place her in a scene visually throughout the story. In order to do so, you need to be able to answer the following questions.

- Is she tall or short?
- Is she blonde, dark, or red-haired?
- How is her hair styled? Is it long, straight, curly, boyishly cropped?
- Is she slim or rounded? Athletic or petite?
- What colour are her eyes? Are they large or small? Wide-set or close together? Are they round, almond-shaped, slanting?
- Does she wear spectacles?
- Is her skin that of an English Rose or olive tinted or black?
- What sort of clothes does she prefer? What styles and colours? Is she a power-dressed businesswoman or an unsophisticated tomboy?

Your heroine doesn't have to be a conventional beauty. Every type of woman has their own special appeal, and each hero will find a different one devastatingly attractive. Think how boring life would be if we all looked the same. That goes for novels too.

It can help to find a picture in a magazine that looks like your heroine. Cut it out and keep it where you can see it. Or note down your answers to the questions above. You may think you will never forget what your heroine looks like but it has been known that a heroine who has green eyes in Chapter One suddenly has brown ones in Chapter Five.

Using description in the novel

When a novel is written from the heroine's point of view, it can be difficult to give a description of her appearance in a way that doesn't seem forced. The idea of the heroine looking in the mirror has been used so many times it's now a cliché and best avoided.

Don't give a complete description in one solid lump, try to scatter it through the text in smaller sections that build up to a complete picture. You can do this through dialogue:

'I'm glad I had my hair cut,' Maria declared. 'This short bob is so much easier to deal with.'

Or you can use action:

'Lucy used a soft brown eye shadow to emphasise the shape of her clear green eyes, then applied mascara generously to her long, fair lashes.'

Use sensuous, vivid language to describe your heroine's physical appearance, for example, saying 'her blue eyes were like bright sapphires' or 'long hair, the colour of the leaves of a copper beech hung down her back.'

Remember to use clothes, jewellery, shoes and accessories to add to the picture.

Finally, remember that appearance also includes a character's mannerisms, the way they move, and any habits that reveal their personality. Does your heroine stride along confidently? Does she bite her lip if nervous? If you can see her clearly, you will describe her so that she will seem truly alive, not just exist on the page.

Heroine's Background

Your heroine is not born on the first page of your novel. If she is really to come alive and be a rounded, believable character, she has to have a 'history', a past life, family and friends, joys and sorrows that existed before the story you are telling even starts. You need to know all the details of that history, even if some of them are not directly relevant to the plot of your book.

To do this, you should create a profile which includes:

- Her age
- Her occupation and her educational background.
- Her parents – what do they do? Are they still alive? If not, what happened to them?
- Any brothers and sisters? Names? Are they older or younger? What do they do? What sort of relationship do they have?
- Was her childhood happy or unhappy? Why? How has this affected her?
- Has she had any other romantic relationships in the past? Were they happy or not? How did they end?

Getting inside your heroine

Once you have established what your heroine looks like and what her background is, you need to understand her personality. If you know just what makes her tick you will be able to write convincingly about her, no matter what happens to her. Whatever sort of a scene you put her in, you will know exactly how she will react.

When you want to build up a rounded picture of your heroine, you need to consider the sort of thing that will make her sympathetic to your readers, but at the same time you don't want to make her so perfect that she is unattractive. You need to know something of how she thinks and feels in order to make her behaviour consistent and believable.

To do this you should think about the following:

- What does she believe in?
- What does she want most out of life? Career success? Love? Children?
- What makes her angry?

- Is she easily angered and emotional or calmly rational? Would she confront the hero or try to reason with him?
- What is she afraid of? People? Heights? Mice? Nothing?
- What would she do anything for, no matter what? Her family? Her child? Her job?
- What are her best points? And what are her faults?
- What are her favourite things – books, films, music, animals? And her favourite places?
- If she was stranded on a desert island, how would she cope? And what would she miss most?

By now, your character should be taking solid shape in your mind. If you write a 'biography' of her before you even begin on Chapter One, you will never have to pause to wonder what she would do in this scene or how she would react to a particular event.

If you know her well enough, she may even be able to dictate some of the action for you. You may have decided that you want a scene to go a particular way, but understanding your heroine will tell you that she wouldn't do any such thing. That knowledge will also suggest an alternative approach to the problem. If you really get under her skin, you will never have to wonder about her motivation or her actions. She will come alive on the page and be a believable, rounded character not just a cardboard cut out.

Now read the KEY POINTS from Chapter Two

KEY POINTS
CREATING CHARACTERS – THE HEROINE

- Look at the novels you have read to see how the author makes the heroine become the 'gateway' into the story. Consider the ways in which the reader is made to sympathise with her.

- Consider the various types of heroines in a variety of books in order to see how different modern heroines are from those in the past.

- Browse through a dictionary of first names, selecting some at random, and note down a description of the type of person that name makes you think of

- Practice short 'pencil portraits' to describe the physical appearance of these characters

- Create some 'character biographies' giving your heroine's background, her likes and dislikes and inner feelings.

3

CREATING CHARACTERS – THE HERO

If the heroine is the reader's guide into the story, the 'eyes' through which the action is seen, the hero is the character most likely to be remembered. Think of Mr Darcy in *Pride and Prejudice* or Heathcliff in *Wuthering Heights*. A memorable hero can outlive the time or place in which a novel was written and appeal to women all over the world for centuries to come.

Creating a believable hero

Everything that you learned about creating a rounded character for a heroine also applies to the character of the hero, but with some very vital differences. Obviously, he is male and so will behave and think rather differently to the heroine. He also has to be the type of man with whom the heroine can believably fall in love.

And not just the heroine. The reader also needs to fall in love with him. In order to make this happen, he must be charismatic, forceful and very memorable. A romance is a fantasy and a hero a dream man.

But this doesn't mean you can create a one-dimensional cardboard character who rants and postures throughout the book before tossing a marriage proposal at the heroine on the last page. No modern woman is likely to stand for that in real life and they don't want to read about it either. Your hero must have emotions, dreams and vulnerability just as much as your heroine.

Names

Look back at what you learned about the importance of names for your heroine, and try the same exercise for the hero. Remember that a hero needs to be strong and masculine, so choose names that make you think of those traits.

Also bear in mind the period in which your book is set. There are fashions for names as for anything else. In the past, Algernon or Wilfred would have been more popular than they are now but Wayne or Elvis would be totally inappropriate. You have to consider whether a name that perhaps sounds 'wimpish' now might have been more forceful in a different period.

Some authors have a fondness for the most outlandish names to label their heroes with. Names like Rock, Brand or Vargen have a strong, powerful sound, but you need to be careful that your quest for something different doesn't lead you to something that your reader might find quite ridiculous.

Short, forceful names often work well, or names that can be shortened to a single syllable. Or you can use a nickname if you like. But again always consider your hero's surname and how well it combines with his first name.

If you're really stuck, look at the cast list for a play or film, or the list of credits for any television programme. Think about the people you might think of being 'behind' such names. Would they be heroes or villains? What would they look like?

Appearance

Think of a romantic hero and the words 'tall, dark and handsome' immediately come to mind. Not every hero needs to fit such a description, it would be dreadfully boring if every one of them was identical, but any man described in this way starts off with a natural advantage in the hero stakes.

Mr Tall Dark and Handsome is attractive all over the world and the idea of his being dark fits well with suggestions of mystery or a dark past, elements that can be very successfully combined in a hero's make-up. But the description can also be something of a cliché, an easy shorthand that makes for a stereotype hero so you will need more than just that to give him the charisma he needs.

And remember that 'tall' is only a relative term. If your heroine is five feet ten in her stocking feet, then a hero would need to be well over six feet to be described in this way. But to a woman who is a petite four feet eleven, any man six or more inches taller would merit the same description.

But heroes can come in all shapes and sizes. Don't be misled by the covers on many romance books where they all seem impossibly handsome. Inside they might be described rather differently. I have read books where the hero wears glasses, is scarred, is shorter than the heroine, but none of these distinguishing features ever appeared on the cover.

If you do decide to go for something unconventional and more original for your hero, be sure you can carry it off. There is no reason at all why a short, heavily overweight, bald man, or a rebellious punk with dyed hair and a pierced nose cannot be a hero. But you will have to accept that you have restricted their appeal from the start and you will need to work that extra bit harder on their character to compensate

Background

You need to know every bit as much about your hero's background as you do about your heroine's, in order to flesh him out as a believable figure.

Review the section on the heroine's background and ask yourself the same sort of questions about your hero, all the time thinking about what sort of a man his past life would have turned him into. In older romances, a hero could have got away with being mysteriously dark and cynical with very little justification, and not much of an explanation as to *why* he was like that. Today's heroes have to have good reason for their cynicism or whatever.

Mystery

In some senses, a hero is always a mystery to the heroine. She doesn't know how he feels about her, why he is behaving in a particular sort of way. But a real hint of intrigue, a shadow of some past event, or failed relationship adds that extra touch of excitement to finding out more about him. It enhances the progress of the love story between the two major characters if it is matched by a movement from dark into light, leaving behind the past and its sorrows or disillusionments.

The Alpha Male

The Alpha male is the traditional macho hero. He is a tough, confident character, usually a self-made man and often in a dangerous occupation. He is supremely confident, ruthless and hard-edged, a high achiever who controls the lives of others, eliminates any obstacles in his path and is predatory and forceful. Physically all such heroes stand out by their looks, height and demeanour. The Alpha Male is a challenge to the heroine. She has to stand up to him or he will walk right over her. But it can be difficult to make him appear attractive. Too much arrogance etc, and he can come across simply as a brute, a man no woman would even tolerate, let alone want to marry.

If you want to create this sort of a hero, you need to make sure that he has private vulnerabilities, hidden weaknesses or secrets he is not prepared to reveal in order to make him appeal to a modern audience. This is why you need to know your hero from inside out. You need to make him ambiguous, at times he must play the villain as well as the hero, but if there isn't the possibility of that other side to him you will lose the sympathy of your reader.

The 'New Man'

The moves towards greater equality for both sexes have opened the way for a different, gentler, more thoughtful type of hero. This caring, thoughtful character is a considerate lover, a good father, a supportive partner, with tolerance and a sense of humour, the sort of man who has been described as an ideal, in real life.

But in fiction there can be a very narrow line between being a gentle man and being a wimp. If you prefer to write about such a hero, you need to be sure you give him plenty of inner strength, a 'backbone' that will make his character as appealing as the more obvious attractions of the Alpha male. He needs to be strong in a different way.

The conflict between a heroine and this New man hero will usually be less intense, less antagonistic than that between her and the Alpha hero. It is often imposed from outside, by forces beyond their control or the circumstances in which they find themselves – on opposite sides in a war, for example.

Making an entrance

In many novels, particularly the shorter contemporary romances published by Harlequin Mills & Boon, it is a good idea
To get your hero to make an appearance as early as possible, and usually to make his arrival as dramatic as possible. In a short book, you have only a limited number of words in which to let him make an impact and no space for sub-plots or lesser characters. In a longer book, such as a family saga, you can allow yourself a more leisurely approach.

Some psychologists believe that in encounters with new people we have just met, most of our impressions, and often lasting ones, are formed within the first four minutes. If you keep this in mind when you are introducing your hero to your heroine, it could help you give him more of an impact.

Try and think about meeting someone for the first time. What things did you notice most about them? Did you get a favourable impression of them or just the opposite? What was it about them that gave you that feeling? The way they dressed? Spoke? Acted?

Once you have your hero 'on stage' you should try and keep him with your heroine in order to emphasise the developing relationship between them. Again, this intense focus is most needed in a shorter romance, but even in a longer book if the hero is away from the action for too long his influence on the plot can be weakened.

Ambiguity

I've already mentioned that, at times, the hero must play the role of both the hero and the villain, but this ambiguity must be handled with care. At times he must appear to be a danger to the heroine, whether financial, physical or emotional, and because the novel is usually seen through her eyes, if she is mistaken in his motives then the reader will be too.

But if you know your character from the inside out, you will know the things that are hidden, which the heroine has yet to discover. You will know what is really motivating him, the past hurts or mistakes that are blinding him or sheer lack of information that is misleading him so that how he *appears* to be behaving is open to another very different interpretation. You cannot have him behaving as an obnoxious brute simply because 'that's what romance heroes do'.

Now read the KEY POINTS FROM Chapter Three

KEY POINTS
CREATING CHARACTERS – THE HERO

- Think about the heroes in the novels you have read? Which ones particularly appealed to you or which ones did you hate? What do you think makes a memorable hero?

- Look at the ideas in the KEY POINTS FOR Chapter Two. Try some of these again, but this time from the point of view of the hero instead of the heroine.

- Think about the differences between the Alpha Male and the New Man. Which would you prefer to read about?

- Match them with some of the heroines you've invented and consider what points of conflict might arise between such characters.

- Imagine some action or behaviour on the part of a hero that would alienate your heroine. Now invent a motivation or explanation that would give that same action a very different interpretation.

4

DIALOGUE

Why is dialogue so important?

Try to imagine a novel without any conversation between the characters. The same story could be told, but in a much slower and far less exciting way. Long chunks of narrative distance the reader from your characters. They lack immediacy, the real sense of drama, of being present at the events as they take place.

Show, don't tell

One of the most important rules of writing romantic fiction is: 'Show, don't tell'. If you get your characters to voice their feelings, what's been happening to them, their hopes and dreams; it will have much more impact than simply recounting them in narrative.

Consider the following passages:

1. Lucy sat down abruptly, stunned by the news that Mark had been married before. Mark swung round to face her, unable to understand her shock. He had only been married for a very short time, and the relationship had never really worked. It had all ended very bitterly and he never planned on repeating the experience.

2. Lucy sat down abruptly.

   'I'm stunned! You never told me that you'd been married before.'

   'Why does it matter so much to you?' Mark swung round to face her. 'So I was married once, only for six months but that was quite long enough. It didn't work out. We ended up hating each other and I have no intention of ever repeating the experience.'

Which of these gives you a sense of actually being present at the scene? And which gives you a clearer impression of the character of the man involved and his feelings about his brief marriage?

Dialogue gives your characters a chance to speak for themselves. And it allows your reader to discover facts for themselves, rather than being told them by the author. It puts the sparkle into your narrative which could be very flat without it.

What can dialogue do?

Used in the right way, good dialogue can do any or all of these:

- Provide information
- Move the story along
- Create an emotional mood and add pace, tension and variety
- Enable the characters to reveal themselves to other people in the story, and so to the reader.
- Claim reader attention and set the story or a new part of it in motion.

Provide information

By putting information into your characters' mouths, you eliminate the need for long passages of narrative. For example, if you let your heroine relate what has happened to her you keep her centre stage and in the present where a narrative account would diffuse this focus and slow the pace.

Move the story along

Dialogue is not just small talk or idle chatter used to fill spaces on the page. It should always serve some purpose. Look at some of the novels you have read and study some scenes of dialogue to see how things are at the beginning of the scene and what has changed at the end.

What has been said could change the heroine's whole perspective on how the hero has behaved or reveal the identity of 'the other woman', or simply prove that the hero is just not prepared to listen so that she gives up in despair.

But dialogue should not just be page after page of speech. This can be as boring as any lengthy narrative and it can become difficult to work out just who is speaking. There is also the problem of the characters becoming nothing more than 'talking heads' so that the conversation is carried out in a vacuum, with no references to the physical reality of who is speaking.

To avoid this, and bring the characters back into focus, make sure you give them things to do or gestures or movements that give your reader a visual image of them

For example:

Mark touched Lucy's shoulder gently.

Her hand shook as she lifted her glass to drink from it.

He frowned thoughtfully as he got to his feet.

Create mood and pace

There is often a lot of emotional tension between the hero and heroine in a romantic novel, but it would be a mistake to think that this can only be revealed in constant arguing. A diet of just one type of conversation can be as boring as eating the same food over and over again.

Tension can often be communicated as much by what is not said as by the words that are actually spoken. So a conversation about a business deal can stretch out a heroine's nerves because she really wants this man to say how he feels about her.

This sort of scene can also generate a very different emotion, that of sexual tension where the conversation is matter of fact and businesslike on the surface but the undercurrents are clear to the reader if you drop clues as to how your characters are feeling:

'Perhaps we could discuss the details over lunch?' Mark said with a smile that made her toes curl.

'Lunch?' Lucy assumed an expression of careless indifference. 'I'm afraid I already have an appointment.'

The fact that Lucy 'assumes' an indifferent expression reveals that this is very far from what she is actually feeling.

Finally there are scenes in which the conversational mood changes almost by the second, perhaps going from confrontational to calm, to seductive and finally to passionate in a way that has your reader hurrying to find out what is going to happen next.

Reveal character

This is where 'show don't tell' really matters. Think about people you know and how they speak. How do the words they use, jokes they make, favourite phrases, reveal the sort of person they are? Words are the most important way we can show what we are feeling, or conceal the truth from someone.

Make sure your characters speak in a way that fits with the people you know them to be. If your hero is an important, highly successful businessman, is he likely to say, 'Oh Marykins, please would you be a sweetie and type this letter for me'? And don't just say 'He had a wickedly sarcastic tongue.' Show him using it on his secretary or the heroine. That way, the reader can decide for herself if he is deliberately being nasty or trying to goad her into thinking hard about something she is convinced is true.

If you really understand your characters you will be able to show what they *do* and *why* they do it and know what they *say* and *how* they say it.

Claiming the reader's attention

If you have had a break in the story, say at the end of a chapter, and you are picking it up again at a different point, using dialogue is a very good idea. It immediately sets the mood, grabs the reader's interest, and makes them want to read on.

This can be particularly helpful if some time has passed since the last event and the scene you are currently describing. Instead of trying to find a way to say that ten days had passed, you can get your character to do it for you:

'I can't believe that it's only ten days since Mark Fletcher came back to the village!' Lucy sighed. 'Just look at the way he's turned things upside down in that time!'

Starting a new section, chapter, or even a whole book with a line of intriguing, provocative or downright mysterious conversation is also a good device for curing procrastination or even writer's block. Once you've got those words down on paper, you're right there in the scene with your characters and the need to explain why they were said or what happened as a result will soon carry you along.

He said, she said

Overuse of 'he said' or 'she said' will be repetitious and soon grate on your reader. One way to tackle the problem is to go through a thesaurus and come up with as many alternatives as possible. You can use 'he shouted', 'she declared', 'Lucy whispered,' etc. And an adverb – cheerfully, unhappily, indifferently – will also communicate the mood.

But if you write your dialogue convincingly, it can often be possible to do away with any such dialogue tags altogether.

If the words a character uses are appropriate, there will be no need to explain how they said it.

For example:

'How dare you set foot in my house after what you've done!'

'Lucy, please forgive me. I had no right to say that.'

You should have no difficulty in deciding just how these words have been used.

If you are not sure about your dialogue and whether it sounds believable and realistic, try reading it aloud. If you can't read it easily, or if it sounds stiff and wooden, it will soon become obvious and you will know your work needs revision.

Using appropriate language

As well as the dialogue needing to be appropriate to the character who uses it, you must be careful to make sure it also fits with the time in which you are setting your story. Language changes so quickly that it can easily become dated in the space of just a few years. If you are writing a contemporary love story this is particularly important as an old-fashioned tone will put the reader off.

Beware of using trendy words that may only have a very short vogue of being fashionable and will sound as very dated very quickly. Think of slang like 'groovy', 'swinging', or the description of someone as a 'dolly bird'. Phrases such as these belong to such a particular period they sound odd in a different setting.

Unless, of course, you are using them deliberately to reveal a particular sort of character. What would you think of someone who called you 'Old chap', or described something as being 'top hole'?

Now read the KEY POINTS FROM Chapter Four

KEY POINTS
DIALOGUE

- Show, don't tell

- Dialogue should provide information, move the story along, reveal character, create emotional mood and pace, or claim the reader's attention.

- Dialogue should fit the character and be appropriate to the setting and the period of the book

- Read your dialogue aloud to hear if it sounds realistic and fluent.

- Avoid over-use of 'he said' or 'she said'.

5

PLOT AND CONFLICT

Page turning quality

A romantic novel could be described as a book in which the course of true love does everything except run smoothly. In many ways, the actual romance between the hero and heroine is really the plot of the novel, while the story in which they are involved is a subplot, but if you are to keep your reader interested and involved, you need other events to give your book that all-important PTQ – *Page turning quality*

Originality

There is probably no such thing as any truly original plot. Most novels, particularly romances, rework themes and plots that have been written over and over again. Obviously, a romance novel has to follow the basic 'boy meets girl' plot mentioned earlier. So how can you make your story interesting and appealing?

What an editor is really looking for is an individual 'voice'. If the boy meets girl plot is the bare bones of a novel, it is the fleshing out of those bones that makes the story come alive. It is the touches of individuality, the way the author imposes his or her personality on the skeleton of the story that make it come alive to a reader.

Characters dictate a plot

Many beginners spend a long time agonising over a plot, trying to think of an interesting idea, before they start to think of the characters who will take part in it. This is really doing things the wrong way round. You can end up imposing your plot on characters who are quite unsuited to it.

If you have spent time building up a profile of you characters and you know them inside and out, you should find that they can dictate your plot for you. You put them together with a basic setting or some sort of catalyst and see what happens.

It should be like introducing two people you know very well to each other. You would know if your friends would get on or not, and what possible points of conflict would crop up between them. It's the same with your characters. You introduce A to B, asking yourself what would happen if . . .? Light a fuse and stand well back!

What should a plot do?

Obviously, a plot tells a story, it is a series of connected events resulting from the situation in which the main characters find themselves and from their personal response to that situation which lead to a climatic conclusion.

In a romance novel, your plot has to answer three basic questions:

1 Why are my hero and heroine attracted to each other?
2 What is keeping them apart – that is, what is the main conflict?
3 How will they resolve this conflict?

The answer to the first question should be easy if you have thought about your characters. You will know what draws them together, what qualities they will discover in each other that will lead to them falling in love.

The answer to the second question makes up the bulk of your story. It is that 'what' that provides the essential conflict that keeps the reader turning the pages.

From the moment your hero and heroine first set eyes on each other, your reader will know that they are destined to be together. It is wondering how they get to that happy ending together with the suspense that comes from the fear that this time they might not make it that keeps them involved. There has to be some problem that the characters must overcome before they can give in to the attraction they feel and commit themselves to a lifetime together.

Conflict

If the point(s) of conflict between your two characters are to keep them apart for the length of a book, which is at least 50,000 words in even the shortest novel, it has to be something worth disagreeing over. It can't just be an instant mutual dislike or a total lack of communication.

Instant dislike dragged out over almost two hundred pages or more soon seems like nothing more than a bad-tempered sulk and loses you reader sympathy immediately. And no one is likely to believe that an intelligent modern woman would break her heart over a problem that could easily be tackled if she and the man she loved simply talked about it.

For example, the 'Other Woman' is an over-used source of conflict that it is difficult to use in any sustained way in a modern novel. Any liberated heroine who is told that her hero has been seen with someone else is much more likely to march up to him and demand to know what he was doing with X rather than packing her bags and leaving.

For this type of problem to work as a source of conflict, it needs to be combined with some other, inner fear of the heroine that would lead her to believe her man was being unfaithful.

There are two types of conflict: *Internal* and *external.*

External conflict.

This is when the conflict between the characters arises from events or forces outside them. External conflict can arise from loyalty to others – parents, or country, for example. Or from mistaken beliefs – that the hero is responsible for some problem the heroine has.

The most obvious example of this sort of conflict is in Shakespeare's *Romeo and Juliet* where the feud between the Montagues and the Capulets is what keeps them apart and ultimately creates the tragedy.

Internal conflict

Internal conflict arises from the character's personalities and their reactions to each other. They are usually emotional origin and are resolved by learning more about themselves or each other or discarding inappropriate beliefs.

A hero who has been badly hurt and who learns to trust again, or a heroine whose own lack of self-esteem leads her to see slights where none are intended both go through internal conflict. In Shakespeare, this sort of plot is shown in *Othello*, where the central character's own mistrust of his wife and his jealousy are what drives the conflict.

Turning old ideas on their heads.

If you can't think of a new idea that excites you, try looking at old, well-used plots in a new light to give you fresh inspiration.

For example, the idea of a heroine working as a nanny to the hero's child has been written many times. But what if the positions were reversed and the nanny was male, his employer female? Why would a hero take on such a role and how would the heroine react?

The same approach can be used in the plot where a secretary goes to work for a famous author, or where all the hero wants is someone to pretend to be his wife or fiancée for a time.

Too much plot

You should be careful not to overload your novel, and your characters, with too much plot, particularly in a short book. If something is always happening it can overwhelm the reader and distract them from the central point of the novel which is the developing relationship between your hero and heroine.

In order to avoid this happening, remember to include some 'getting to know you' time into the story. It is not enough just to have one overwhelming attraction between the hero and heroine; they need to have sound reasons for actually loving each other too. Love at first sight is fine as a lift-off point, but if it is to be the foundation of a lifetime together, it needs to be built on secure ground.

Remember that non-stop arguing and verbal sniping is *not* conflict. The dislike and dispute between the main protagonists have to come from the real conflict that drives them on.

Sub-plots

You need to be careful how you use lesser characters and sub-plots so that they don't complicate and confuse the main plot, especially in a shorter novel.

Sub-plots can be offshoots from the main plot, perhaps involving another member of the family, or a friend. But they must not take over from the main storyline. Each one should have a beginning, a middle and an end, and they should be integral to the main story. If they are woven into it carefully, they can:

- Strengthen the main conflict.
- Help explain and deepen the central characters
- Enhance the main story
- Illuminate differences

  When creating secondary characters or plots, approach them with the same care as you would your hero and heroine. Avoid stereotype plots and clichéd characters. They should have a reason for being in the novel and a purpose to serve.

Now read the KEY POINTS from Chapter Five

KEY POINTS
PLOT AND CONFLICT

- Characters dictate the plot

- Ask yourself: Why are my hero and heroine attracted to each other? What is keeping them apart? How will they resolve this conflict?

- External conflict comes from events and sources outside the characters. Internal conflict comes from within, from their personalities and reactions to each other

- Be careful with subplots Don't let them overwhelm or muddle the main storyline.

6

VIEWPOINT

Whose point of view?

In a novel, the *viewpoint* is the perspective from which the story is seen or the character through whose eyes the events are revealed.

There are several different types of viewpoint. The ones that are most commonly used and which are most appropriate for romance fall into four categories.

1. Omniscient
2. First person
3. Third person
4. Multiple viewpoint

Omniscient

Another name for this is the 'authorial voice'. This is when the author recounts the story and so is able to watch all the action, no matter where it happens, and can see into the minds and thoughts of every character in the novel.

Using this viewpoint means that you can describe any scene that happens at any time or place. You can tell one series of events and then recount another set of actions that happened somewhere else at exactly the same time. You can give your reader information that your characters do not possess. You can even warn the reader of things that are about to happen. For example:

'Lucy need not have worried. Help was already close at hand.'

But using the authorial voice reduces the reader's involvement with the characters. It means that they are kept outside the action, reminding them that they are reading fiction and so can mean they are less caught up in the events. It can be used to establish the setting of a scene before moving into a heroine's viewpoint.

First person

This is the most easily recognised viewpoint. It reads as if someone is telling the story, using I, me or my. The reader looks through the eyes of the storyteller, seeing all the action and every other character through them. *Rebecca* and *Jane Eyre* are famous novels written in the first person.

First person can be very dramatic. It gives direct access to every thought and feeling your central character experiences. But it can also be very limiting. Your reader can see only one approach to events, and the narrator cannot reveal anything that happened when they weren't present. They can't describe anything that happened while they were asleep, or unconscious, or just out of hearing. This means that other characters may have to give long descriptions of events in order to keep the central narrator informed.

Third person

This is the viewpoint that is most often used in writing romance and is perhaps the easiest one for a beginner to use. It is usually described as 'third person subjective' because while actions etc are described in the third person ('Lucy walked out into the crowded street', or 'Mark brought the car to a halt outside the house'.) the events are seen from the perspective of the characters involved.

Everything that happens is filtered through the thoughts and senses of the character whose viewpoint is being used which, in a romance, is usually the heroine. Even description of a scene can be processed in this way.

Lucy's heart lifted as she reached the house. Wood Cottage might be only a small, squat building, with shabby blue paintwork, its garden overgrown because she never had time to tackle the weeds, but to her it was home.

The reader sees the cottage through Lucy's eyes, giving both a factual description and some idea of her character and feelings.

Multiple viewpoint

As mentioned earlier, romances are usually written from the point of view of the heroine, so that she is the reader's 'window' into the story. But there is a growing trend for giving the hero's point of view as well. Sometimes the whole novel is told from the hero's viewpoint, but more often both the hero and the heroine's perspectives are used which gives a multiple viewpoint. *Wuthering Heights* is a classic example of a story told from multiple viewpoints where the different narrators all add their personal opinion of the central characters.

Multiple viewpoint gives the writer an opportunity to show both sides of the story, to reveal the hero's interpretation of the action, and to give the reader information that the heroine is not aware of. But it also makes writing rather more complicated as each different viewpoint used must be kept in character and reveal the individuality of the person involved. Events or conversations or other characters must be seen through the eyes of the protagonists in a way that shows the differences between them and their personalities. It is best not to use too many different viewpoints at once. This can muddle the reader and diffuses their involvement in the story, spreading it thinly amongst so many characters.

Using viewpoint

When using viewpoint as a writing tool, you should consider the following points:
1. You should find out whether the publisher you are aiming your novel at has a preference for a single or multiple viewpoint. The reading you have done will help you here.

A 'confessional' story for a magazine would be written in the first person, but this would not be suitable for a category romance.

2. Viewpoint should always be in character and you should never tell anything that the character who is to be your 'eyes' couldn't possibly know.

3. Use names carefully. You should use the version of a name that your viewpoint character would be likely to call another person. For example, Lucy would think of her mother as 'Mum' or something similar, while Mark might use the more formal 'Mrs Monroe' or 'Liz Monroe', or even 'that Monroe woman'.

4. Use language appropriate to the viewpoint character you have chosen. If you are writing from a multiple viewpoint, the language used by a male character would be very different to that used by a female. Which of the following sounds more like the way your hero might think:

She'd been seeing that damn actor again, in spite of her promise. It was written all over her deceitful little face.

Or

He was sure that she'd been seeing that actor again in spite of having promised not to. The expression on her face gave her away.

5. A viewpoint character can express the emotions they are feeling, but they cannot *see* themselves unless they are in front of a mirror or a shop window. So you can't say that Lucy's face went white with shock, but you can express it through the sensations she is experiencing by writing 'Lucy felt all the blood drain from her face, leaving her skin cold as ice

6. Changing viewpoint reveals your characters' feelings and helps you show changes in their mood and reactions to each other. It can be used to explain reactions that are ambiguous and lets the reader in on secrets that other characters don't know. This gives your reader the thrill of

knowing what your hero really meant as well as seeing the misinterpretation the heroine has put on his actions.

Switching viewpoint

If you do decide to write from a multiple viewpoint, you should be careful about changing from one character to another. If you do it too often you can confuse your reader and weaken their involvement with the story. You should always make it clear whose viewpoint you are using.

Remember that a character's viewpoint will be physical as well as mental. If your hero is taller than your heroine, she may have been looking up at him. If you then switch to his point of view, he will now be looking *down* at her and any description should be written from that perspective.

The easiest way to switch from one viewpoint to another is to do so at a natural break in the text, at the end of a chapter and the beginning of a new one, for example, or when time moves on in the story as in this example:

'Goodnight, Miss Monroe,' Mark said coldly, heading for the door. He'd had enough of her bad-tempered sniping for one night and if he stayed any longer he might just do something he'd regret later.

A double space indicates the passage of time and a change of scene.

Perhaps she'd gone a bit far tonight, Lucy reflected as she got ready for bed. She'd really laid it on with a trowel, and if she was honest Mark hadn't fully deserved it.

With more experience, you can learn how to weave both your hero and heroine's viewpoint into the story so that they exist side by side without the need for breaks like this to show where one starts and the other ends.

Now read the KEY POINTS from Chapter Six

KEY POINTS
VIEWPOINT

- Consider the novels you have read to see what viewpoint they use. How is it achieved and how effective is it?

- Try writing short passages from each sort of viewpoint. See what advantages and disadvantages each one has.

- Write some scenes from the viewpoint of a heroine and then write the same one from the hero's viewpoint using different language and attitudes.

- Practise changing viewpoints either at the end of a chapter or when time passes between scenes.

7

SENSUALITY

Going beyond the bedroom door?

Before you get very deeply into your novel, you need to decide
something important. You have to ask yourself whether you
are going to write something that is restrained, with a chaste,
innocent heroine, or whether your novel is going to be a more
passionate story with what are usually described as 'steamy'
passages describing the physical relationship between your
characters.

In any story of the developing love of a man and a
woman, the sexual attraction between them plays a vital part.
No one would believe that your hero and heroine are truly
destined to be partners for a lifetime if they don't feel an
overpowering physical response to each other. Many, if not all,
of today's romances deal with this aspect of the relationship in
a way that no longer stops firmly this side of the bedroom
door, and contrary to what some critics would have you
believe they have been doing so for years.

So how far do *you* want to go?

Once again, your reading of other novels will help you decide.
If you enjoy reading raunchy novels, then you'll probably enjoy
writing them. But if you find that such scenes embarrass you,
you'll be uncomfortable about putting them into your own
work. If you try to force yourself, the words will sound stiff
and awkward, the opposite of the sensuality that is aimed for.

You don't *have* to put in sexual scenes. While there is no
doubt that the present trend is for sexy novels that sell very

well, romantic fiction always has room for a wide range of approaches. But whichever way you decide, be sure that you are aiming your work at the right publisher and the right strand within their output. If you study the difference between *Mills & Boon Modern* and *Mills & Boon Tender*, for example, you will see that what is appropriate for one would not suit the other.

Contemporary or historical

Think about the period in which your novel is set. If you are writing a contemporary romance, then you need to give it a contemporary feel. Whatever your personal feelings, modern young women regard a sex as a natural part of a relationship with or without marriage.

Your heroine is not going to convince anyone, particularly younger readers, if she doesn't feel some strong physical emotions where the man of her dreams is concerned. If anything, the problem with a contemporary novel can be to give convincing reasons for her *not* to go to bed with her hero, rather than the opposite. But you should always be guided by your characters. A naïve eighteen-year-old from a country village would have a very different response to a sophisticated divorcee of forty.

But in a historical novel the considerations will be quite different. In the days when loss of virginity and the fear of an illegitimate child meant social ruin, women had to be very much more careful, no matter how passionately they felt. Your heroine needs to be true to the time she lives in as well as to her own nature.

You are writing a romance

Perhaps the most important thing to remember when putting the sensuality into your novel is that you are creating a *romance*. You are not writing erotica, though your story may have many erotically charged moments.

The reader is looking for a story that can range from delicately tender to highly passionate encounters with anything in between. What they *don't* want is a scene that reads like a mechanical making-love-by-numbers, or anything that comes close to pornography.

They also want love scenes that develop naturally out of the story you are telling. A string of sexual encounters strung together with only the briefest excuse for a plot is not a romance and will prove very unsatisfactory to most readers.

Emotional tension

When thinking of the scenes that give a book its sensual impact, many beginners make the mistake of thinking simply that sensuality equals sex. More often, it is the fact that the *anticipation* of lovemaking builds the excitement and gives a story that all-important Page Turning Quality mentioned earlier. Sexual tension sizzles as much because of what *doesn't* happen as because of what does.

You should think of the development of any love scene as something like lighting a spectacular bonfire. You need to lay it carefully, starting small and then adding more fuel steadily until it becomes a blazing inferno. That way, it has more impact. If you pour petrol over it right at the start and set light it will very soon burn itself out.

It is also important to include the emotional elements, not just the physical. Your reader wants to know what is going through your heroine's mind, her emotional responses as well as what is happening to her body.

All the senses

Whether in an actual lovemaking scene or not, the descriptions and reactions in your book should bring in all the senses in order to build up as physically solid a picture as possible. Appealing to the five senses will let your reader experience what your characters are experiencing.

- **Sight** – Describe the place where a scene is taking place, the clothes each of them are wearing. Use colour, texture, fabrics to make it live in your reader's mind. Use the weather or their surroundings to reinforce or contrast with their mood – for example, a day of sadness contrasted by a bright, glorious sunny day.

- **Hearing** – The hero's rich deep voice or the heroine's softer, lighter one. Change the way they speak to fit the scene in which they are - tight with tension for a fight or huskily whispered words of love. Music, laughter, the wind in the trees or rain on a roof.

- **Scent** – The most obvious one is perfume for your heroine or perhaps a hero's aftershave. But there are other more natural ones – wood smoke, crushed mint, roses in full bloom, the air after a storm, freshly brewed coffee. What about the deeply personal scent of someone's skin or hair?

- **Taste** – As well as the taste of any food or drink, there is the taste of the hero's lips on the heroine's mouth or her skin against his tongue. Think of the tang of salty air when you're beside the sea. Or other, less obvious tastes such as that of fear or the bitterness of disillusionment.

- **Touch** – Two people who are falling in love want to touch each other all the time. But each caress will be different, depending on the mood of the scene. Think of firm clasp of hands at first meting, a kiss on the back of a hand, the urgency of deep passion. Bring in the contrasts of textures: a silk dress, a leather jacket, the rough stubble on an unshaved masculine face, polished wood or the tickle of grass against the skin.

    Using one or more of these senses in combination will bring a scene alive. If you find it hard to think of anything beyond what your characters *look* like, close your eyes and try to imagine a scene. You should find that the loss of one sense heightens your awareness of the others.

Values

It has already been mentioned that the sexual scenes in your book should reflect the age in which the story is set. To see how this works, consider how you would feel about a hero or heroine who smoked heavily. In the past this might have been seen as the height of sophistication, but a modern reader would consider such behaviour irresponsible and unhealthy.

Just as historical characters have to reflect the moral considerations of their times, so a modern hero and heroine must be shown to be aware of today's sexual problems. It is no longer possible to leap into bed with the nearest available person without considering the possible consequences. Romance stories may be escapism but they don't exist in pure fantasy land where they are in an unrealistic vacuum.

Promiscuity isn't likely to be an attractive trait in any character. AIDS and safe sex have to be considered, as does the problem of protection from an unwanted pregnancy. What would you think of a hero or heroine who was totally irresponsible about this? But it needs to be done subtly if it is not to intrude into a love scene and destroy the mood completely.

Finally

Sex sells books, but all the sex in the world won't put that vital spark into a novel if the story is so old and tired your reader knows exactly what's coming or the characters are so cardboard and one-dimensional she just doesn't care about them.

Now read the KEY POINTS from Chapter Seven

KEY POINTS
SENSUALITY

- Write at the level of sensuality that you feel happy with, otherwise it will seem forced and wooden.

- Write about what is appropriate to the period in which your novel is set.

- Consider the values of the age about which you are writing.

- Remember you are writing a *romance*, not erotica.

- Emotional tension comes from anticipation and from what is left out, not just from what is stated.

- Appeal to all the senses to build up as physical a picture as possible.

8

BEGINNINGS, MIDDLES AND ENDINGS

The importance of a good beginning

Have you ever watched someone browsing in a bookshop? How do they go about choosing a novel they want to buy?

First, the cover or the title catches their eye and makes them take the book off the shelf to consider closer. Then they read the 'blurb' on the back. If they are still interested, they open the book and read the first page. Occasionally, they turn to page two, but no more. If they like what they read, they take the book to the counter. If they don't, it goes back on the shelf.

It all takes just a couple of seconds before their mind is made up. In a world where there are thousands of other similar books available, what will make them choose yours instead of someone else's? If your beginning doesn't grab them from the start, they are unlikely to want to read any further.

Beginning well

A good beginning to any novel should:

- Claim the reader's attention – this is the 'hook' that keeps them reading
- Introduce the characters
- Introduce the potential conflict
- Hint at what is to come

Hook your reader

You should try to begin with a bang. Start the story at a turning point in the heroine's life. Perhaps she has a crisis to deal with, financial or emotional, or a relationship has just broken up, or a parent has died. Remember that the story starts before you have even put pen to paper, so ask yourself, what has happened to your heroine before the first chapter starts?

Particularly in the short, category romances like those for Harlequin Mills & Boon, you don't have time to spend long paragraphs giving a poetic description of the setting, detailing the heroine's background and how she came to be there. Such a staid beginning is unlikely to grab your reader and make them want to keep turning the pages

Remember how dialogue can be used to claim a reader's attention. A story that begins with a provoking and intriguing piece of dialogue will make the reader want to know what is happening.

Begin in the middle

This may sound contradictory, but you can get a strong impact if you begin your story partway through, with the change or the crisis that has been forced on to your heroine, and not with a chronological account of how it came about. You can fill in all the details later.

But don't give all the information in large, solid chunks. Spread it through the text a little at a time, that way you can keep an element of mystery that will have your reader guessing and wanting to know more.

Think of the way you would tell a friend about a film you saw last night. If you want them to share your excitement and enjoyment of it, you wouldn't spend half an hour talking about the heroine's life history; you would launch straight into what the plot was actually about. 'The heroine met this guy on a train and they decided to spend the next twenty-four hours together.' Only later would you add, 'Oh, and she'd been married before but . . .'

Middles

A very common mistake that beginners often make is to think about the beginning of their book, know that the ending will be happy, and then assume that inspiration will carry them from start to finish. It is very easy to run out of steam in the middle this way. You can end up with a long, flat, slow middle section or, even worse, the dreaded 'writer's block'.

The way to get round this is to write a novel plan before you begin.

Novel plan – what happens next?

A novel plan is the bare bones of your story, on which you will hang all the details of the plot and character in order to build up a fully fleshed-out story. It helps you know where you're going, what's happening to your hero and heroine, and reduces the chances of running out of steam halfway through.

First, you divide your story up into a number of chapters. This is only a rough idea, so it doesn't have to be strictly accurate. But, for example, if you are writing a short novel of around 55,000 words, you might have around twelve chapters. Obviously a longer book would have more.

Next you write a synopsis of your plot, breaking it up into the chapters so that something important to the development of the story goes into each one. If it helps, you can put each chapter on to a separate page. That way, you can easily add more to it if inspiration strikes.

You can jot down snatches of dialogue or descriptions of possible settings if you think of them. At this point, the structure of your plot is very flexible. If you find that as you write about your characters and get to know them better something doesn't seem quite right you can change it to take into account these new twists and turns.

But the important thing is that you have the skeleton of your book sketched out. It will help to keep your novel on the boil when inspiration flags, and you should never be stuck for what happens next because you have it written down.

A plan will also help you with the pacing of your novel so that the reader's interest in it never flags.

Pace – keeping the reader hooked.

Just as you need to get your reader hooked at the beginning, you need to keep them turning the pages and wanting to read on. Hooks are most often used at the ending of a chapter, leaving the story at some crisis point that will make it impossible to put down. But if they are scattered all the way through the novel they will increase the tension, create suspense and produce that page-turning quality you are aiming for.

Hooks are created by:

- New facts being revealed
- Sudden disasters
- Changes which the reader knows have been coming but the hero or heroine don't
- Complications or obstacles which prevent the characters reaching their goals
- Questions which have to be answered

In the same way as you spread information through the book, you feed your reader a little intrigue at a time. Your plot needs to be like a roller-coaster ride, sometimes going up high to an exciting scene of conflict or passion, or down to the depths of despair and at others travelling along a smoother, more gentle slope so that your reader can draw breath.

Getting to know you

Also in the middle of the book you need to have that vital filling out of your characters so that they can get to know each other. This is when they discover things about each other that makes them fall in love.

Happy endings

Everyone knows that the traditional romance ends with 'and they lived happily ever after'. But just because that is what is expected, it doesn't mean that you can rush through it and so sell your readers short.

A good ending should:

- Create an emotional climax
- Resolve all difficulties
- Explain all misunderstandings
- Sum up the characters
- Most important – it must satisfy your reader

The final resolution

The ending is the last time your reader spends with your characters, and just as you wouldn't rush good friends out of the door with scarcely a goodbye, so you don't want to finish your story too quickly.

You must be sure that you have cleared up every misunderstanding and complication you have created. But don't spring surprises on your reader unless you have already laid down clues. If there are a lot of problems and loose ends to sort out, it is usually a good idea to deal with some of the lesser points before the ending so as not to overwhelm your characters.

'But you said. . .'

The run-up to the final pages is often described as the 'But you said. . .' section because the hero and heroine have so much to talk about and misunderstandings to clear up. But be careful that they don't end up just explaining and explaining. Look at the section on dialogue to remind yourself how to avoid them becoming just 'talking heads'.

Romantic ending

You are writing the end to a romantic novel. Your reader has stayed with your hero and heroine through their conflicts and arguments, their hopes and despairs, so now you should reward them by spending some time on the declaration of love that they have been waiting for all this time. As before, don't rush it through, giving everything at once. Your heroine can tease the hero, seeming to need persuasion to say what she feels, or if the hero is the strong silent type she may need to push him into speech.

Endings can be breathlessly exciting resolutions, where happiness is snatched from despair at the last moment. They can be gentle and tender or fiercely passionate, or even humorous. But they should leave your reader on a high in which all their hopes and dreams have been satisfied.

And they must be appropriate to the characters and the plot you have created. It can take several rewrites before you get just the right ending for this particular book. But   it's worth the effort, because if a beginning sells *this* book, then and ending sells the *next* one. It is what lives in your reader's mind and makes her look out for your name on other book covers in the future.

Now read the KEY POINTS from Chapter Eight

KEY POINTS
BEGINNINGS, MIDDLES AND ENDINGS

- Beginnings hook the reader
- Open with impact, at a crisis or a turning point
- Write out a novel plan before you begin
- Vary the pace of scenes
- Make endings satisfying and emotional

9

SETTINGS

Exotic or everyday?

One of the most pervasive myths about romantic fiction is that a romance can only be set in glamorous surroundings, on a desert island or in some other exotic country.

It's true that if you imagine your reader considering the 'blurb' on the back of a book, Barbados has initially more appeal that, say, Bolton, but this does not mean that it's impossible to set a very good and emotionally appealing novel in Bolton, or anywhere else for that matter.

Write about what you know

As with the careers and lifestyles you give your characters, it is a good idea to start out by writing about something that you know well. If the only place you have ever lived is a tiny rural village in Wales, you are unlikely to be able to write about the jet-set life in Monte Carlo with conviction. And you don't need to.

Remember that romantic fiction has readers all over the world. So wherever you set your story, it will be unusual and exotic to some reader somewhere else in the world. It is far better to write with conviction and knowledge so that you create a setting and an environment that seems real and believable in your readers' minds, rather than to try and invent some exotic surroundings that just don't ring true because you haven't got the facts to make them real.

Do your research

If you do decide to set your story in a country that is foreign to you, make sure that you do your research. Nothing is more off-putting than to read a book with an exotic setting that is just not accurate. If you do get facts wrong, people do notice. It spoils their enjoyment of this book and means they are unlikely to want to read another by the same author.

So find out everything you can about the place you have chosen. The best possible approach is to visit your setting yourself, spend time in all the important places, make notes, take photographs. But if you can't do this make use of your local library and read up on the country until you're confident.

You can also write to tourist information offices (enclosing a stamped addressed envelope) and ask for local guides and leaflets. Study the history of a place as well, often the past or local legends can throw up intriguing possibilities that can be woven into your story.

Background

The background of a novel is just that: *background.* It is the scenery against which your characters move and act, but it should never overwhelm them or intrude into the action.

You are writing a novel, not a travelogue. You are telling a story that happens to be set in Madeira, or on a cruise ship. You are not telling the history of the island, or writing a tourist's guide to every port the ship stops at. So you should provide enough detail to make the place seem real but not so much as to distract the reader from the story you are telling.

Professions

A place of work can be a setting just as much as a country or a town. If you are writing a romance with a medical background, you will need to know how a big modern hospital works or the day to day running of a busy GP's surgery if you are to write with conviction. You will also need to have accurate details of any illness or other medical problems you intend to weave into the plot.

As with place, if you are not sure of the facts about any profession you plan to use, you must do your research. You will never create a believable businessman or a dashing airline pilot if you can't provide some facts about what they do, any training they needed to get where they are, the sort of things that occupy their minds.

Romance may be fantasy, but it has to be grounded in fact. Readers like to learn about interesting and glamorous jobs, both for the heroine and the hero, and they like the insights they get to be accurate. Once again, if you don't already know it, read up about it. Ask questions, watch television programmes and find out as much as you can.

Historical

Everything that has been said about other types of setting can be applied to an historical novel. You will soon lose readers if you have a heroine checking her watch in mediaeval times or switching on the electric light in a Regency romance. You need to be as accurate as possible in your facts and use them to give the atmosphere of the time, not to make your story sound like a fictionalised history textbook.

The five senses

The chapter on sensuality showed how to use all five senses in descriptions of people and surroundings. When you are creating the setting for your story, you should use the same technique to bring the place it is set in to life.

Obviously you will describe the physical appearance of the place, the colour of the houses, the trees and plants. But what about the sound of church bell or the cry of birds? Is it a busy, bustling place full of people's voices or calm and quiet? Does it have a particular smell, either pleasant or unpleasant? The perfume of flowers or the tang of the sea? Is it hot or cold? Does the food taste spicy or bland? Are the roads smooth or cobbled, tarmac or beaten earth?

Settings affect the action
Settings are more than just the physical surroundings in which the plot takes place. They can have a powerful effect on the action, either by reflecting it or by creating other dangers and tensions than the ones the characters are already dealing with.

Consider these possibilities:

- If your hero and heroine are on a Caribbean island, are they there alone or in a busy holiday resort where other people can play a part in their story? Does the hero have a private jet so that he can take off at a moment's notice, or will he have to stay there until there is a commercial flight out? Is the heroine there on holiday or working? Or does she live there?

- If the setting is a jungle, this will bring additional dangers to whatever situation your characters find themselves in. These will show very different sides to them than they would reveal in a city or on a beach. Dangers can throw people together or drive them apart. Survival skills can seem impressive or callous depending on how you look at them

- A cottage on the Yorkshire moors in a snowstorm that blocks all the roads is a confining, claustrophobic environment. A relationship could build up very quickly as a result of such close proximity. There's no escape; it's a pressure cooker situation. And what will happen when the snow melts and they are free to go?

Settings and character
The worlds that characters live in shape their personalities and reflect the kind of people they are. They can also be the possible cause of some of the conflict between the two.

- What if the heroine's world is in a small rural village where she's lived all her life and it is invaded by a man with a jet set character and reputation? How is she likely to react? What similarities will there be between the two of them? And what differences?
- But if the heroine is a high-powered businesswoman, a success in her own right, at home in a cut-throat world, she would meet him on very different terms.
- Finally, what if the hero had come from 'the wrong side of the tracks' in their hometown, he's been away for years but now he's back and he's a very different man. How do you think the townspeople would react? And what would be his response to them?

Think carefully about the setting you plan to use for your novel. It could make or break your story. Would *Wuthering Heights* have had the same impact if it had been set anywhere other than the Yorkshire moors? Or could Scarlet O'Hara have been such a memorable heroine if her story hadn't been set against the American Civil War and on the great estate of Tara?

Now read the KEY POINTS from Chapter Nine

KEY POINTS
SETTINGS

- Settings don't need to be exotic or unusual. Better to write with conviction about what you know
- If you do decide to use a foreign setting, make sure your facts are accurate. Do your research
- You are writing a novel, not a travelogue. Background should stay in the background
- A profession or a place of work is a setting too. The details need to be factually correct
- Use all five sense when describing your characters' surroundings
- Settings affect the action and the characters

10

SUBMITTING YOUR WORK

You have finished your novel, and now you dream of seeing it published. What do you do next?

Prepare your manuscript

Any work you submit to either a publisher or an agent should be professionally presented. First impressions count so you should make sure your manuscript meets these standards:

- Good English. No poor spellings, grammatical or clerical errors
- Clear layout
- Readable text. Use a good quality typewriter or printer ribbon, not one that is old and faded. If you had to read hundreds of manuscripts with pale grey print, you'd soon see why.
- Number pages clearly
- As an extra identifying and security measure, use a header with your name or pseudonym and the title of your book at the top of each page. Publisher's offices are full of manuscripts and it is possible for a page from someone else's story to end up in yours or *vice versa*.
- Put all the pages in a simple card folder and hold them together with a rubber band
- Do an accurate word count, either using a computer or by taking an average of the number of words per page and multiplying this by the total number of pages, making

allowances for the beginnings and endings of chapters where there is not a full page of script

- Post your manuscript in a padded Jiffy bag or similar to protect it in the post
- Always remember to include return postage

Publisher or Agent?

Some publishers only look at scripts that are sent to them by an agent. Agents act as filters, weeding out unsuitable novels and submitting only those they believe have a chance. Other publishers prefer to see only a letter and a synopsis so that they can decide if they want to see the whole manuscript.

Do some market research. Go through the *Writers' and Artists' Yearbook* or *The Writer's Handbook* and study their sections on publishers and agents. Choose the ones who state that they take popular or romantic fiction, and submit only what they ask for. If they specify no unsolicited manuscripts, they will simply return yours unread if you send it to them. If they ask for just a query letter, send just that and remember to enclose return postage for a reply.

Introductory letter

If either a publisher or an agent asks for a letter and a synopsis, you need to make sure that you give them all the information necessary to make a decision as to whether to see your work.

Your letter should include:

- Essential information about your manuscript: what genre it fits into, what age range it is aimed at, the theme of the story, a little about your characters, and a basic idea of the story
- Information about yourself as a writer, any previous publishing experiences and successes

- Details of any background you have that is relevant to the novel. For example, if you worked as a stockbroker and your novel is set in the world of high finance, put that in.

Synopsis

The synopsis is your chance to sell your story so it should be as carefully written as the novel itself and polished until you are completely happy. Imagine that you are writing the blurb to go on the jacket of your book when it is published and include all the points you think would attract a reader to buy your book.

Your synopsis should include:

- Details on the hero and heroine, background, career etc
- How they come together at the start of the book
- The setting of the story, whether a country, historical period or professional environment
- The source and nature of the conflict between them and some idea of their individual motivations in relation to it
- How this conflict is resolved
- Brief details of any subplots or secondary themes and characters if relevant
- Write a synopsis in the present, giving pivotal scenes and crises – the highs and lows on the rollercoaster – and how the characters change
- Your synopsis should be about three or four pages, A4, double spaced

After submission

- Be prepared to wait. Publishers receive hundreds of unsolicited manuscripts (for example, Harlequin Mills & Boon receive over 5,000 new manuscripts each year) and it will take time to get round to reading yours. Don't pester the publisher for a response.

- Revisions and rewrites: if you are asked to do any rewriting of your novel, remember that this means it shows promise. It does not mean that once the revisions are done it will automatically be accepted, but at least it is not just a rejection slip. Always be prepared to listen to advice. Publisher's editors know what is selling and what is not.

Surviving rejection

- Persevere. Don't just sit back and wait to see what happens. If you really want to write, start thinking about your next project at once. Working on it will help the time pass while you wait for a decision on your previous one, and if you're already partway through a new story it will be easier to continue than it would be to start from scratch in the face of rejection.

- Be realistic. The proportion of first novels that are accepted is very small. Consider it an achievement just to have written a novel at all. Many people say they 'always meant to write a book' but very few actually get down to starting it. Even fewer finish.

- If your book comes back with just a printed rejection slip, it feels like the end of the world, but you can always try again. If you are lucky enough to have any comment on your work, take note of the criticisms offered and try to apply them to your next project

Getting help and support

If you are not given any criticism of your work, it can be difficult to find anyone who can give you knowledgeable, objective comments. Consider some of the following:

- Join a local writers' circle or a creative writing class in your area. The local further education college or the WEA should be able to supply you with details

- Join a writers' organisation. The *Writers' and Artists' Yearbook* lists the available professional organisations. For anyone interested in writing romantic fiction, the **Romantic Novelists' Association** (RNA) is possibly the best. Unpublished writers can join their New Writers scheme which provides advice and criticism, and there is the chance of winning the annual New Writers' Award. (For the address see Reference Section)
- Pay for criticism and advice. The RNA newsletter often advertises criticism and advice services offered by qualified readers. Or look in *Writer's Monthly* magazine. (Details in reference section)

Finally

Above all else, **don't give up.** Unfortunately, rejection is a fact of life for the would-be writer – and often for the published author too. Many famous authors had their books turned down at the beginning. Even Frederick Forsyth's *The Day of the Jackal* was rejected several times and yet it went on to become a best-seller and was made into a film.

If you really want to write, you'll learn from rejection, pick yourself up, dust yourself off and start all over again. I know it isn't as easy as it sounds, but remember, even the biggest best-seller in the history of printing will never get anywhere at all if it's all still inside someone's head.

The only way you can ever get your novel onto the shelves in the bookshops is to write it down and send it off. It's true that doing that means you risk rejection, but if you don't do it you have no chance at all of success.

Now read the KEY POINTS from Chapter Ten

KEY POINTS
SUBMITTING YOUR WORK

- Make sure that your manuscript is as professionally presented as possible
- Research your publisher or agent carefully
- Submit only what they ask for
- Provide a covering letter and a detailed synopsis
- Always enclose return postage if you want your manuscript back
- Be realistic – rejection happens to even well-known authors
- Accept criticism and advice
- Persevere

11

The 5 Ws (and one H) of Writing Romance

(This is the transcript of a Question and Answer session I did on the Harlequin website (http://www.eharlequin.com). It is reproduced here with the kind permission of Harlequin. Because of copyright issues, I have not reproduced the questions exactly, but have paraphrased them to cover the subject.)

The 5 Ws ? What's that about? Well, really it's anything you want to ask about writing for Presents/Modern - or just Romance in general. The basic plot of a romance - the skeleton on which everything else hangs - never changes. The so-called 'formula' is this: Hero meets heroine. They fall in love but there are problems along the way that need to be resolved. When these problems are resolved there is a happy ever after ending. It's not really possible to be highly original with that. The part of a romance that makes the difference - the bit you can change and make your own - comes into the 5 Ws - Who, Where, What, When and Why - and don't forget that H - How. In Kate's opinion, the most important of those will always be WHY - but she's happy to answer questions about any or all of the others.

1. **WHO?**

Obviously in a romance, the WHO are the hero(H) and the heroine(h). That's so clear and straightforward, it doesn't really need saying - but I have to start somewhere.

The first thing about characters is to choose ones you want to write about. This may sound like something obvious again, but you'd be amazed the number of would-be writers of romance who write what they think of 'typical' even stereotypical romance characters. They think the h has to be a wimpish Cinderella-virgin and the hero a macho brute because they see 'Alpha' as meaning monster. And then they wonder why the ms is returned because the H&h are 'unsympathetic'

So what you're trying to create is a vital, vulnerable and vivacious heroine who will appeal to women who are living in the 2000s not the idea what a romance heroine 'should' be like. She should be modern, realistic, believable.

And the same for your hero. Yes, he can be as rich, macho, powerful, arrogant as you like (that's the fun of writing romance) but he should be the sort of man who, if you strip away all the trappings of money and power etc is still hero material. The sort of man a woman would be proud to be with, who she could trust and respect as well as fancy the pants off. For example - I have a book (The Hired husband) where my hero is at a point in his life when things aren't going right in his business so she's the one who provides the financial support he need - but does he let that emasculate him - no way!

So you need to know your H&h inside and out. You need to know what makes them tick. What their background is and how it affects them. No character ever starts living on page one of a book. They always have a 'backstory' of their own - even if you never tell it. And as those of you who dipped into the '12 points' will already know, you need to give your H&h that vital vulnerability that will put a chink in their armour and make them accessible both to the audience and to each other.

Of course, the most vital vulnerability for each of them is that they can't help falling in love with the other, even if that person seems the worst character in the world to tumble head over heels for.

Which brings me to a question I'm often asked. What is the most important part of why the hero and heroine fall in love? - The most important part of WHY the H&h fall in love - is what is personal to them! That is why you must know your characters inside out. And you need to create characters that your reader will believe belong together, that there couldn't be anyone else for that character.

This is a fascinating question, because if you look around at the people you know, and the people they're married to - even look at your own partner - and ask 'Why?' 'Why are they together?' 'Why did I marry this man?' (yes - I know some times it can be hard to remember - but try!) Love is not only blind; it's also the exact opposite. It sees things in other people that no one else can find. And these days a woman needs more than just a man who can provide financially for her - a lot of the time, she's more than capable of doing that for herself. So you're looking at emotional fulfilment - two halves of a whole - and for every couple, that's going to be very different.

So this is why that question WHY will keep coming back and back. You're looking at your characters and thinking 'What does this person most need?' And it may well not be anything like they THINK they need. That's what makes a developing relationship so intriguing. Obviously sex comes into it in a big way - lust at first sight, is far more common than love at first sight. But from then on it's like peeling an onion - there are layers and layers of the person to discover. And at any point you might discover a discoloured layer, one that puts you right off and stops real love forming right there!

So we're back to that vital vulnerability in your character - perhaps it's one they don't even know they have. And when the other person touches that, it's like scoring a bullseye. There's no turning back..

So, as I've said, and I'm sure I'll keep saying, you need to know your characters and then you'll know just where that bullseye is and how the other person can hit it.

QUESTION:

My heroine seems to be rather inconsistent. How much of a problem is this?

ANSWER:

Your heroine is doing something called growing. At least I hope that's what she's doing.

When we start a romance (as writers that is) we begin with out H&h at Point A in their lives, and then we introduce the falling in love problem to complicate matters and we have to stick with them while they adjust to that and absorb it into their lives and adjust to the changes it brings - and take them right through the Z and The End.

So obviously, the effect this is going to have is going to be a growth curve where your h (in this case) absorbs what is happening to her and how its affecting and changing her life and there's going to be a bit of 'two steps forwards, one step back' movement going on.

So far, so good - if what she's doing is adjusting.

But what worries me is if she's becoming totally inconsistent and behaving in a way that contradicts something of her you started out with. Which I suppose brings me back to that question WHY.

Ask yourself WHY is she doing this. If you and she can give an answer then you understand her mental processes and can allow her a little leeway - but if she's just being wholeheartedly inconsistent and changeable you might need to sit down and get to know her better. Do some deep character analysis - mostly of the question WHY type. Ask why is this happening, why is that. And only when you know what she really feels and thinks can you let her act. Otherwise she could just lead you (and her poor H) a merry dance that no one believes in and eventually the poor guy is going to give up, say 'To hell with it!' and walk off.

I'd say you need to get to know her better and understand her motivations more thoroughly before you let her make another move. Sit down with her and make her write out her CV so that she can apply for the job of being your heroine!

QUESTION:

I'm finding it difficult to make the hero and heroine in my second story totally unlike the ones in my first. Have you any advice on dealing with this?

ANSWER:

About your heroine - a couple of things occur to me

1. Maybe you haven't said goodbye to your first heroine properly yet. This can happen. It happens to me if I start on a new book too soon and haven't got the first set of characters out of my mind yet. You may have to tell you first heroine to go away!

2. You may not know your new heroine well enough yet. Try the CV approach I suggested - sit her down and make her tell you all about herself. But make her concentrate specially on the ways she's different from the first heroine - hobbies, family, perfume she wears - anything - then write a couple of scenes bringing in those facts so you get the new person into your head.

3. Try the Q&A approach - but with your hero. Ask HIM what he likes about this heroine - because she's the one he's going to fall in love with, not the first one - WHY (it's that question again!) does he love her, not the other? Again, note the answers and write a couple of scenes using those ideas

And if all else fails write a scene in which heroine B is doing something that heroine A would never, ever do!

QUESTION:

How do you stop a heroine from being just a mirror reflection of your own character?

ANSWER:

The problem is creating a heroine who is an identity in her own right, not part of you. There are those who would say that everything you write is autobiographical, because we all write about ourselves in the end, but that would be rather limiting. You'd end up with the same heroine time after time after time.

The fun thing about writing is that you can create characters who can do things you can't do - my heroines have been able to stick to a diet, been artistic, been able to sing - and best of all, they can think of great comebacks when the hero is being nasty - in the sort of situation where I'd only think of the perfect thing to say hours later, when he'd gone.

We're back to knowing your H/h well again. There seems to be a common strand here – writers who are okay with their heroes but not their heroines. Is part of this because you're all putting yourself into them? And the hero is pure fantasy? So all the answers about getting to know your heroine apply here too. And if you're finding that the h is getting too close to home, then make her something you're not. But the most important thing is to be inside her head. To ask yourself, not what would I do in this situation - or even just go with what seems sensible, because that will seem sensible to YOU. What you have to ask is 'Okay, h, what would you do here?'

Spend time building up a picture and a character study of your h - until you know her like you'd know your best friend. I'm sure that if you were to ask yourself what would - - - - (insert name of best friend here) do, you'd be able to answer, even if it was very different from the way you'd act. That's how you want to be with your heroine.

Once again, you could try working with a character who is so unlike you - confident where you're shy/artistic where you can't draw a straight line/dark where you're fair etc to create a totally new person and then put her into scenes and see how she would react.

QUESTION:
What about the 'backstory' If there are things in the past that are important, how do you weave these into the present day plot?

ANSWER:
Backstories are always difficult to fill in. You're quite right - you don't want to overload the reader with facts and details at the beginning so that they feel they're being given a history lesson and not reading a story about the present. But if you leave it too long then the poor reader can end up totally mystified, confused and not understanding what's going on at all. At it's worst, this can mean that you lose that vital sympathy that the reader must have for your H&h.

So you need to fill bits in - and really the earlier the better. Unless there is some important detail that you must keep secret, it's best to let the reader know it as soon as possible so that they can get on with the story of the present - which is what they're reading for. This doesn't mean that the H&h need to know everything, but help your reader out! Halfway through is getting late. I'd say you need to go back over what you've written and see if you can put in some bits and pieces of information - in a thought for example - so that there isn't so much to explain later. As I said, the only reason for hanging on to something is to use it for the most impact if it comes late - like in my book His Miracle Baby- when the details of my hero's past have been kept from the heroine and she finally learns them and realises why he's behaved as he did.

But always remember that it is the current love story the reader wants, so you want to get that information in as soon as possible. Break it up if you can - give a bit here, a bit there. If you're using dual POV you can have the person concerned remembering. And if it isn't absolutely vital that this stays a secret from the other, then let them tell each other some of what happened - they can always stop short and say 'I don't want to talk about it any more' if you don't want to give too much away. But they're going to have to tell each other eventually and you don't want to clog up the ending with too much detail of the part of their lives that was in the past.

QUESTION:

I can't seem to end my story, no matter how much I write, I still have more ideas and its length is way over the word count. How do you keep within the required limits?

ANSWER:

The problem is with writing for a series romance is that it needs a strong discipline. You have to meet - and not exceed - the word count stipulated for the line you're aiming for. Unfortunately, writing more won't get you any extra points - you will simply be told to cut it. And that can hurt. I speak as someone who once had to cut 15,000 words from an early manuscript and it felt like cutting my arm off.

Now, really, with a romance there is an obvious ending - the H&h declare their love for each other and fall into each other's arms. But your H&h won't get there. So you need to ask why.

Why don't they feel that the story is complete and they are ready for that HEA (happy ever after)commitment? What is missing in their story that you need to put in to bring them to the right conclusion? Perhaps they're thrashing around, looking for what they really need and just filling in time with the rest of it. Or maybe it's that you can't bear to part with them.

Or perhaps what you're writing is 'filling' - interesting events that you're enjoying writing but which don't actually move the plot along very far - and if you're not careful then filling becomes padding and padding weighs down a book, makes it slow and doughy and soggy in the middle. Again, I've done this - I had a book with an opening set at a fancy dress party, where my H&h were dressed like Jane Austen characters. I spent a lot of time making them speak to each other like Jane's H&h from Pride and Prejudice and had a lot of fun with it but then I realised it wasn't going anywhere and it all had to go in the bin. It broke my writer's heart but it didn't fit with what I was writing and the genre I was writing it for.

Or perhaps you're putting in too many secondary or even third place characters, characters who might be happier in their own plots in their own books but in this one are taking too much of the limelight from your H&h. I know some category line, and mainstream fiction give you more words, more scope for other characters, but in category romance, those word counts are there for a reason. They are planned to give the reader a paced read and the skill is in keeping the story to the limit.

In the end, I'm afraid you may just have to bite the bullet, and decide that you have to end it if it's going to be for a particular category. Decide on an end - jump ahead to it if necessary, and only allow yourself to write scenes that move you towards that. It's sad but true that quite often a writer isn't the best judge of her own work. What may seem to you like pages of wonderful story might be just that padding to an editor.

And the crunch comes with the fact that no book is ever going to be accepted if it hasn't got a beginning, a middle and an end.

QUESTION:

Do your characters ever totally amaze you with something you weren't expecting?

ANSWER:

Oh boy do I know what you mean! Yes - don't forget you're talking to the writer who once stopped dead in the supermarket and said 'So that's why you did that!' to the empty air. When they do that to you, you need to note where it happened - I have a notepad by the computer and I just put 'Liam said she was like his mother' or whatever and the page number. Then I can find it easily if I need to. Because sometimes this is a flash of inspiration and your characters are alive and taking over - and if that's so then the plot will develop wonderfully from there and you can go back and tweak the beginning into place. Because in my mind beginnings are never set in stone. You're just starting out, finding your way. The plot you may think you have could develop into something else and then you'll have to go back and tweak.

But it's equally possible that this is just a bit of bad behaviour on your characters' parts and later you'll want to go back and tweak that bit - which is why noting down helps because you can find it easily.

So if they do that, don't just take their word for it. We're back to my favourite question - WHY did they do that? If it fits or throws up an interesting character trait that you think deepens their personality, work with it. But always remember who's boss. There's nothing worse than a pair of ill-disciplined characters running wild and doing all sorts of crazy things because their author didn't impose a little control when it was needed.

QUESTION:

I find that secondary characters are easier to write than the main ones. Why do you think this is?

ANSWER

I totally agree with you on secondary characters - they have so much less to lose - they can be weird or crazy or mean or downright cruel because it isn't essential that the reader has the same empathy with them that they must have with the H&h. I still smile to remember the aunt in Anna Adams' Unexpected Babies -who stuck tape on her face to smooth out the wrinkles. You can definitely make secondary characters much eccentric. But in a category romance you have to be careful that the secondary characters don't swamp the H&h and their story. Superromance for example gives you more scope for this, but in a Presents/Modern say, you need to get that tight focus on the H&h and secondary characters can dilute it.

But yes you can bring them in and they can be great fun to use -and can be very helpful. They can show very different sides to your central characters - ones the other main character might not see normally. Or, as I said to, you can use them to help tell some of the backstory, or to move the plot along by their actions. But whatever they do, it's definitely as you said, they just have this job to do and then they can bow out again, so if the reader hates them or finds them too crazy it doesn't matter and you can have fun creating them.

Of course sometimes you can create a secondary character and then find that they've grabbed your imagination and need a book all of their own. That's what happened with the last book I wrote - the hero's halfbrother won't let me rest until I tell his story. Gio is nagging me to get on with his book.

QUESTION

What about the darker sides to characters? Do you ever show these and if so how? What do you have to be careful of?

ANSWER

Speaking personally, I like to deal with flawed characters, ones who have that touch of darkness, sadness, even guilt about them. That's why revenge is a great theme - and in the process the would-be revenger learns a lot about themselves and comes to realise they need to change. I've written some very bitter heroes who have had to learn to come to terms with things, and some very prejudiced heroines who won't see straight.

When you're writing about these sort of characters, you always have to keep in mind a couple of things - one, you are writing a romance, so you are heading for that HEA ending when all is resolved. So you need to known that the problems you've set up can be dealt with, sorted out, and answered in the timespan/word count you have at your disposal.

Two, you don't want to lose the reader's sympathy with your characters, so if you are going to give a character a negative side to them or a negative trait, then you need to give them very good reasons for having that there. You only have a short novel in which to redeem them and make your reader believe that they have a chance of happiness with their hero or heroine. I've seen heroes with prison records - but you need to be careful with what they've done because there are some crimes which readers could never, ever forgive even the most repentant of heroes. And again you need to think very very carefully about WHY they ended up there. Anne McAllister, for example, writes about wonderful cowboys who are rather flawed at the beginning but they end up making up for it brilliantly by the end.

I agree that you don't want to have them change into an angel overnight - totally unbelievable so, as I said you need to set up the reasons - usually in their past - why they are behaving like this. Then as soon as you can you need to hint at possible changes, a slight softening. It doesn't happen all at once, and it can be something that goes in two steps forward, one back - then forward again. And of course you don't transform them into saints - after all, a flawed human being is a much more rounded one, more believable too. So, for example, you could have your arrogant, domineering hero apparently totally submissive, seemingly conquered by his love for his heroine, then just at the last minute showing a flash of his old arrogance to show that he's not completely demasculated.

2. WHERE?

Where? Seems obvious, but maybe it isn't. WHERE? Is setting - that's the obvious bit - but let me tell you a story:

I was doing a talk on writing Romance and afterwards a lady came up to me and said could she ask a question. She said that she had travelled a lot, been on a lot of cruises etc so she knew she could write a brilliant romance. All she had to do was to decide which place to set it - so did I think the cruise in Egypt or the Mediterranean one?

Me: But do you have a story? Characters ?

Lady: Oh no - but that won't matter will it? It's the exotic setting they want

When I picked myself up off the floor I managed to gasp that she was going about this back to front but she wasn't listening. She had her exotic setting and she'd be fine, she thought.

Now, Presents/Modern novels have a reputation for being set in romantic and sophisticated - and, yes - exotic - places and I've set mine in Greece and Venice and a fictional Arab kingdom - but check the books out - there's a lot of variety in how much detail a place is given because, the setting is really an address where things happen. So even if your characters are in some foreign country - or just in the heroine's backyard - or some small cottage in Cumbria, it's what's happening that matters and the setting can be a plus but it shouldn't be all.

I learned this the hard way - setting a book in Malta, which I'd visited and loved. I wrote at length about the island - until my editor said in exasperation, 'This is a romance, not a travel guide!' and cut thousands of words of my lyrical descriptions.

And - consider how much effect the setting has on the mental state of the H&h - because different settings have such different atmospheres. A tropical island might sound wonderful - but H&h can't get away from each other easily except by plane or boat. A cottage in Yorkshire where they're snowed in (like in Fiancée By Mistake) has an even more claustrophobic atmosphere. But if you put them in a big city like London say then they will have plenty of space to get away from each other and plenty of distractions - so you'd need to find ways of bringing them together this time. And what about that Arab kingdom, or anywhere similar - where the heroine doesn't know her way around, or speak the language - she's immediately much more vulnerable and the hero has more advantage because he's on home territory. Or vice versa.

So you need to think about what your setting is adding to the story. Even just that heroine's backyard has its own personal atmosphere because in a small town/village if everyone knows everyone else's business then H&h might need to hide their relationship - or, alternatively, flaunt it.

QUESTION:
Romance often seem to be set in exotic locations? Is this vital?

ANSWER
. It can add to the atmosphere, it can give a sophisticated feel, or the opposite, to the story, readers like a foreign setting - but 'it's only an address'. The spotlight should be concentrated on the H&h and their story - not a travelogue.

QUESTION:
Can you change the scene too often in a book. You don't want to stay in the same place all the time but what would be too much?

ANSWER

The answer to your question is really 'Do what suits your book'. I have written books - the stranded in the snow type for example - where there was one setting and one only. Then I've written ones where the H&h move around. Her Secret Bridegroom began in Venice - a couple of locations there - then back to England - heroine's home - then to the Lake District - then back again.

What you don't want to do is to fuddle the reader with too many places and too much description. As I said, what matters is the romance, and you don't want to distract from that. Settings that are sketched in lightly don't intrude. So what you're looking at to see if it's working is - does the spotlight stay on the H&h or does it focus on the settings?' Of course, you have only a short book here, so switching locales every couple of scenes can get confusing. But if you have reasons for them being where they are and they move only now and then you shouldn't have any problem. A good rule of thumb is to try and think what setting best suits the scene you want -for example a physical seduction scene would not fit in a busy shopping centre(but then again . . .)

QUESTION

Can you have any sort of setting? Or are there some that just won't work? Do you have any special ones you like to use? And do some setting sell better than others?

ANSWER

Great question. And the answer is a resounding yes. A skilful author can make any location work. Lynne Graham once had her H&h locked up in a huge metal container (they'd been kidnapped) for a long part of the book. Not exotic. Not glamorous. Not even very comfortable - and not much privacy - so she used all those elements to build the relationship. There are settings that go in and out of fashion. My mother had a friend who wrote for M&B in the 60's - she set lots of books on ships/cruises. Those are not so popular now. Will the sheikh/Arabian stories continue to be popular in the current situation? Again, we're back to the concentration on the H&h and making the setting what it should be - that other word for it - background. And it should stay in the background.

But I think from what I said above that you'll see that an exotic - or even a romantic setting isn't vital, because it isn't what makes the book. What makes it are the characters and if they work then it could be set in someone's garage and never move from there. Though I suspect that a suggestion of the setting would make a reader pick up a book on impulse if it hinted at escape and warm sun in the middle of November.

My favourite locations? Well - I have to admit to a fondness for the 'trapped in a cottage on the snowy moors' story. Partly because I'm a northerner who loves the Yorkshire moors, but also because I love the claustrophobia of it. The way the H&h can't get away from each other and have to face their problems, like it or not. I find that if I have a setting in a place I really love (like Malta - see above) I get caught up in the memories and describing it and lose sight of the story - so a lot of my favourite places I don't use. But as to how they've correlated with bestsellers? That's difficult. Constantine's Revenge sold really well - but was that the fact that part of it was on a Greek island? Or was it just that the hero was Greek - and it was in a great mini-series with other great writers? I think the hero part will win out - see - it's what I said. Concentrate on the H&h and the setting should be like the decorations at Christmas - attractive and setting the atmosphere, but not part of life.

QUESTION
What sort of work is involved in choosing a particular setting? Do you have to do a lot of research?

ANSWER

Researching - well, now that I've said how the background is the background, I try to do research to give me a flavour of a place and then sketch it in in fine strokes to give that same flavour but not too much detail. I have several excellent reference guides to places I know I'll use often - Greece, Italy, Spain - with lots of facts, colour photos, food details etc. I also read lots and lots of travel magazines and if I find ones that specifically mention a Greek Island, say or a Spanish coastal town, I clip out and keep the article. Photos are very good because I can have them in front of me when I'm describing a scene or send them to the art department to use. I also try and learn a few phrases in the language so that I can use that to give authenticity. Luckily I know someone who is married to an Italian, someone who is Spanish - all very useful.

QUESTION

Is it more difficult if you set the book in a large, impersonal city where they can be widely separated, rather than a more confined location where they can't avoid each other so easily?

ANSWER

Yes, I know that problem - hero or heroine has walked out on the other, vowing never to see him/her again - and now how do you get them back together again? Why do you think I like the snowed-in scenario? That usually means they can't get away too easily. Special tricks? Well - once again, you need to look at your H&h and see if you can find the answer from them. Sometimes they have given you a clue earlier on. For example – Fiancée By Mistake - she walked out on him, but she had told him that she worked in a travel agent's in a certain part of London so he came to find her. Or Constantine's Revenge - which is all about trust - when Grace really needed someone she could trust she knew she had to find Constantine again.

But to be honest, I might let my H&h get away from each other in the book - and then meet up unexpectedly - say, at a party or in an office - or be invited to the same place by a friend who is matchmaking. But when it gets close to the end, to the final black moment before the reconciliation, I often keep them together - just. They might be in different rooms in the same house or he might be on his way out in a fury when something happens to stop him. I think if you look at their characters, you'll find that one of them is likely to come chasing after the other to confront the situation - that always brings them together. What is really happening in the background is that they might be in conflict but they also know they can't bear to stay apart so then they come up with the most weird and unbelievable explanations why they've come to find the other person, just to justify it. So it doesn't always have to be totally believable anyway

QUESTION
If I don't have any knowledge of anywhere exciting, will I have to try very hard to make everyday settings more interesting?

ANSWER
Have you tried 'looking' at somewhere familiar through your character's eyes? He/she may see things very differently from you. For example, a rich, powerful, maybe even aristocratic hero might see a small town as either a shabby, one-horse kind of place - or then again he might see it as a wonderful homely place, the sort of town he grew up in and was happiest in. An artistic heroine might appreciate the architecture, old buildings etc, while a restless, ambitious heroine might see it as a sleepy backwoods hick town from which she wants to escape. They'll each centre on something different in the same place.

Or why not have the best of both worlds - and have the sort of town that's 'on your doorstep' but fill in new and different details by creating the place in your imagination?

I'll add on a story that shows how you don't have to have the experiences you give your H&h so long as you research carefully. I was doing a talk and at the end, as I always do, I asked if there were questions. One lady said yes, she had a question - how did I fit in my amazing social life. I was confused - stunned would be the word - I don't travel far and wide or visit exotic places (these boards are about as exotic as it gets!) When she explained , it turned out that she had read a book in which my heroine went to a hunt ball and because of that she thought that I regularly went out to such social functions. No way! So use your imagination. Almost all the places I describe are part real, part imagination - and as I said you only need to sketch in a background for your readers to be able to add their imaginations to it and make it real.

QUESTION:
So many books seem to be 'reunion' stories- where the hero and heroine knew each other before. Is it the present day story that's most important or what happened before the book starts?

Great question. It gives me the perfect lead into:
3. WHEN?
This is another of those ones that seems obvious - so equally obviously, it isn't!

WHEN? When does this story take place? If you're writing a contemporary romance, then it takes place in the 'present day'. If it's a historical romance it takes place in 1066 or 1385 or 1642 - or whenever you've decided to set it. Right?

Yes - as far as it goes.

First things first - that Present Day bit (and the historical one too) You should always remember that you are writing about heroes and heroines who are appropriate to the climate of society of the day. For example - 1950/1960s heroes - and often heroines too - could smoke like chimneys and no one minded. It was seen as sophisticated rather that dangerous. My very first paperback hero in Game of Hazard smoked. I wouldn't let a hero do that now. This also has repercussions for the love scenes. Years ago it was understood that a 'nice girl' would say no and that was that. These days, it can be harder to explain why a heroine says no than why she would say yes. And would you consider a man heroic if he didn't at least suggest using a condom? There are all sorts of other things that modern science has changed - birth control - paternity tests. The suspicion a hero might have had a child that was/was not his that once could have lasted throughout the book can now be dealt with in one chapter.

Equally please if you are working on a historical book, make sure you get your facts right! I have heard of would-be writers who have medieval knights worrying about germs or Mary Queen of Scots telling Boswell to get a maid to make him a sandwich.

So that's aspect of it - next is the details of WHEN? If your story is set in winter then you'll be writing about cold days, early nights, late dawns - summer in Greece might sound wonderful but could be almost too hot to do anything - spring in Scotland is not the same as Spring in Cornwall (American/Canadian/Australian readers insert names of cities in the far North and the far South as appropriate). You don't want to set an outdoor seduction scene in the heather on the moors in January - believe me - you don't! You need to get your facts right again - weather, flowers, crops, festivals, holidays etc. These can all be brought in to add to the colour and the reality of the story but only if you get them right.

Finally WHEN? In your characters' lives is this story happening? It's often said that it's a good thing to start your story at a point of crisis in your H or h's life. Say she's just lost her job or her fiancée has been unfaithful - or he finds he needs his estranged wife for some reason. So what has brought them to this present day in which they're living? What has happened either just immediately prior to this or in the distant past to make them the person they are?

And this is where the reunion question comes in. I've said before that your characters aren't just born in the moment they appear on page one. They have past lives, past histories, past experiences, past lovers. Obviously this has all affected them and made them who they are. The most evident of these is a story where your H&h were together before the book starts - either married or just as lovers or even just friends. Then they have a past history to refer to - and usually to clear up and explain before they can move on in the present. But also people who have never met before bring their own personal baggage with them into any new relationship. You need to take that into consideration.

One other thing - if your H&h do have a past history - then you need to work on the balance of telling that backstory and making sure that you focus on the present day relationship. You will also need to decide whether your story works better by beginning in the present day and occasionally flashing back to the past or starting with the earlier stage of the relationship and then jumping to one/three/nine whatever years later. Always remember that it is the present that the reader wants and don't overload them with the past.

QUESTION:
Isn't it true that a story that unfolds quickly (in a week or two) can be much more intense than one that takes perhaps a year or more? The couple need to face up to things more quickly.

ANSWER:

Timespan is a great question too. Some books just roar through the plot at speed and barely need a week in which to sort everything out. And others need a more careful unravelling to work them out. And yes that's one of the great things about the confined space like the snowed in cabin that forces your H&h to look at themselves and at their actions and face up to it. Because if you think about real life, usually one of the problems is that of getting the warring couple together even to speak to each other. And it can't just be like in a soap opera when people are always storming out at the end of a scene.

This is what's partly involved in pacing a novel. So - if I can bring in that reunion question here because it is relevant to this - if your H&h have a past history, a failed marriage or relationship then the book tends to have a shorter time span - they both know what the problem is, they just need their heads banging together to make them face it. And if you put in some reason why they're brought together - a sick child, a bankrupt business, a huge debt - then working on that should bring out things about which they made mistakes in the past. Their shared history will also resurrect good feelings they once had for each other and so they can fall back into love

.   If however your H&h have only just met they need time to get to know each other, time - for a start - to have a reason to have any conflict at all. If you simply start with 'they hated each other on sight' with no justification for that feeling you're going to convince no one. Plus it's more likely that two single people will do more of the getting away from each other that has to be dealt with in a story. And of course, the idea of falling in love at first sight is a tricky one. Falling into lust is one thing - but then real love comes with some knowledge of the person so you need time to find that.

Now here's where I do what might seem like a cop out. Because I have to say that your timespan should be what suits your book, your H&h, your story. I've had characters fall in love from scratch in one week (Flirting With Danger) but then what they went through in that time provided the sort of hothouse atmosphere that forced the relationship and definitely (certainly for the hero) proved his feelings so much that there was little room for doubt. The again I've had books that have lasted a year or more. The Hired Husband does that because that's what the H&h have set themselves.

And of course, it does depend on whether your conflict is internal or external. External - where the problem has been caused by someone else, can usually be cleared up pretty fast once you let your H&h discover who lied/stole/cheated/set up the problem. Then they realise that the other one is innocent and the barriers to the relationship can be removed. But internal - where the problems are in themselves, their feelings, their mistakes, can be more difficult. It takes time to regain trust, even if love is there.

So what you need is to look at how your H&h are going to prove to each other that they do love them. If it's a dramatic move like, say the H risking his life for the h, then that is going to come about more quickly. If it's a slow, careful, winning back of trust then it's going to take longer. So you need to look at your conflict and see if it can be resolved fast or not.

One other point - if you impose a limited timespan on your H&h then they have to get a move on to get themselves sorted out. So if, say, the terms of a will mean that they have to get married within 6 weeks then you have a natural framework for your story. You can create your own framework - the nine months it takes from conception to birth of a baby - the need to have whatever done 'by Christmas' or before an elderly parent dies or whatever. The shorter the framework, the faster the pace of a book tends to be.

QUESTION:

Why are the reunion stories so popular? Are they easier to write?

ANSWER

I think most of your answer is given already - - basically it's easier if your H&h have a past and so a ready made conflict and lots of past knowledge of each other and shared memories to draw on. But writing the same type of story all the time is no challenge at all so I try to do something different when I can. Desert Affair starts with the H&h setting eyes on each other for the first time. The one after that (The Duke's Secret Wife) obviously has a reunion story. The one I'm working on now is about a couple who have a very short but intense shared history- they've known each other just a year.

Each sort of story has its own challenges, its own problems. I like tackling each one as it comes - and again it's the characters who set up the situation and so dictate most of how the story goes.

QUESTION:

Does it matter how long it takes for the relationship between the H&h to develop into love? Are there any rules about the length of time in a book?

ANSWER

I hope most of what I've already said covers what you wanted to know. If you go back to Who? It's clear that just as in real life, so all characters are different. Some people fall in love once - bang! Hit on the head with it and never look back - and this can last a lifetime. Others, perhaps because of something that happened in their past, a messy divorce etc, are more reluctant to give their hearts or to trust. The answer is usually in the feelings of your characters (again!) What you want to do is to give the true value to what your H&h are feeling. If there is a deep, bitter pain, a hurt that has scarred so badly it feels it will never heal, you are belittling that feeling by having a swift and almost instant cure and falling into love with someone else, or even the person who hurt them that way. Or you could have the very quick head over heels into love followed by panic stricken 'Ohmigod what have I done' sort of doubts. One of my shortest time span books – Game of Hazard - takes just 3 days for most of it - but then in the last chapter or two the action has to slow slightly, letting both H&h draw breath, get out of the snowed in cottage and back to real life, and think about their feelings - and then decide that yes they really do love each other.

I think a lot depends on the circumstances in which your H&h meet as well. It's that holiday romance thing. If they meet on some tropical island and fall madly for each other in the week of a holiday then they need to come out of that idyllic place to put their relationship into the real world. But if they're meeting out there in the real world and dealing with problems that come at them then they would get to know each other in a very different way and at a very different pace. What you need to set up is a time scale that feels right for your characters and the type of people they are, giving enough time to test that feeling, either in a fast dramatic way or in a more paced learning to love way as fits both them and the plot you've set up. There are no hard and set rules - just that you want your reader to believe at the end that this couple could have a chance at happy ever after because of what they've learned about each other.

QUESTION:

I never know exactly when to begin my story – whether I should start in the past and then bring it up to date, or write the past in 'flashback'.

ANSWER:

That's so true - once you find the beginning - the real, the right beginning, you just know it - but finding it can take several false starts. Sometimes I just plunge in and go back to write the beginning later. As to how much background - the best rule of thumb is as little as you can get away with. You don't want to confuse people by having them wonder just what is going on but really you can just sketch in the backgound. This is usually one of the things that really is best shown not told - ie with dialogue if at all possible.

4. **WHAT?**

WHAT happens in your book? At its very basic level, this is what makes up the plot - your characters' story. The nuts and bolts of 'They meet - this happens - and then that happens - and then that happens - and then this explains it all - and they sort it all out and they live happily ever after.'

Now in a romance it is very, very difficult to be at all original. You all know that. You've read enough to see that the most you can manage is perhaps an interesting twist on a well-worn theme. So you panic because you don't have a new idea under the sun. Well - don't. Some highly intellectual critic whose name I always keep forgetting once put forward the theory that there are only ever seven different plots in the whole of fiction, and all stories are simply reworkings and variations on them. So if that's the case you can't really ever hope to be desperately original - but you can be unique - you can create your own voice, your own type of heroine, your own hero. Look at the books you've read. See how different authors have this - a Holly Jacobs book couldn't be an Anna Adams book - or a Kate Walker. And even in one series - like Presents/Modern - a Lynne Graham heroine is totally different from Michelle Reid's or Sandra Marton's.

So you decide to be yourself. Not a pale copy of anyone else. Harlequin aren't looking for 'another Kate Walker' - they've got one. What they are looking for is someone who puts their own stamp on a book, who tells the traditional stories in her way. And that means bringing in any life experiences that can help you create a believable setting, attractive characters, a passionate conflict. If you don't know anything about - say - the world of a huge newspaper office then either research it or don't write it. If you get it wrong, people will know.

But more important - and by now you should be expecting this - is the WHAT is happening underneath what is happening. You know the sort of thing - the hero may be telling the heroine that he wants her to work for him as a nanny, but underneath what he wants is to watch her with the child and to try and test out if she really is the sort of person he's been told or the person his instincts are telling him to go with. Or the heroine is saying 'I don't want anything to do with you, I want you out of my life and never come back ' when inside she's thinking 'I love you. I'll never love anyone like you, but I can't admit it because . ..'

We're back to peeling away that onion as I said earlier - taking off layers and layers until you get to the real truth. What is really being said. What is really happening. And of course, because this is a romance, what is happening is that your H&h are falling madly in love- no matter how hard they try to deny it. Nowhere is this more important than in a lovemaking scene.

Okay, so in a lovemaking scene it's very easy to say WHAT is happening - on one level.

After all, we all know just what is going on in the bedroom. There's little new for anyone to write about there. But to me what really really matters is the before and after. Which is where that most important of all the senses - the mind comes in.

Because what really helps me write a love scene is the way that I've built up to it. The events that have happened before this development - the mood of the moments before and the way that this has moved into the couple making love. I try to make each love scene different and to make sure that each one moves the relationship along. Because, let's face it, sex does change things between people.

You can never look at someone in the same way once you've been intimate with them. And angry sex is very very different from slow, gentle, giving sex. So you need to look at the scene as it builds.

What is happening between your H/h just before? What mood are they in with each other?
 Are they both totally involved or is one of them fighting their feelings like mad?
Are they happy and confident together or is there a lack of trust maybe that would put a sharp edge of unhappiness on to the wonderful physical feelings?

Finally - never forget the 'after' as well as the 'before' and the 'during'. To me, a love scene isn't just put in to show the physical passion between these two people or to create a sensual atmosphere - though obviously that's important. But in the course of the story you need to show how that moment of intimacy changed things between them - made them feel more secure, or totally lost. Whether it convinced her that he loves her - or quite the opposite. How will they feel 'the morning after' - or whenever the passion recedes and they have to face each other again? Because- and there's no pun intended here - lovemaking strips humans naked. They reveal so much more than their bodies to each other - and if the scenes before give you the build up to the lovemaking scene, then the moments after are what will lead you into the next stage of your story and the next stage in the development of their relationship.

QUESTION:

Are there any forbidden topics? Or ones that you don't think can be dealt with in a romance?

ANSWER:

Taboos? Hmm - well that's a tricky one. For a start it does tend to depend on which line you're writing for. Romance - or Tender in the UK - is a very different approach to something like Intrigue. I would have said that murder, rape, incest would be difficult themes to work on - but in Intrigue it seems as if every second heroine has had a husband or child or husband and child done away with - or there are murderers hunting the H&h. I've touched on incest - but the suspicion/fear of not the actual fact in the Temptation Game. And Michelle Reid's The Marriage Surrender deals with the aftermath of rape. Charlotte Lamb's Guilty Love deals with a hero who has been in prison for apparently murdering the heroine's husband and she has also touched on reincarnation and the heroine holding the hero prisoner (though not in the same book!). Child abuse (in the past) has been in books such as the one Sandra Field wrote about an abused hero. Lynne Graham has dealt with surrogate motherhood and Susan Napier who had sperm donation in one of her books. And Emma Darcy has dealt with a hero whose wife is on a life support system. Anne Mather has heroes much younger than her heroines. All in Presents/Modern Romances.

Obviously, Presents/Modern is my field and the one I know best so I can't say with any authority about the other lines, but the field is far more wide-ranging than most people suspect Jennifer Taylor for example has a mixed-race marriage in one of her Medicals. Not the central H&h relationship, but it's there - as it damn well should be. Oh, and of course Constantine has a friend who is gay in Constantine's Revenge - and right back in 1986 my hero had a black brother-in-law.. The problem is one that many writers just starting out will find that what is acceptable to an established writer is not so easily taken on from a newcomer.

I have a personal rule - if I can't do a subject justice, then I won't write about it. I never ever want to do a serious subject a disfavour by writing it inaccurately or too lightly. So I haven't written about a disabled character or someone who's blind for example because I don't know enough about it.

The problem is that you can have a topic that most people would think would be fine but experience has taught Harlequin that such books don't sell well - revenge is now back in favour but I remember within the last 10 years an established author being told that revenge just wasn't popular. Other 'non-sellers' have been discussed - Musicians, actors, Scotland, beards, red-headed men (though I remember a very very sexy redheaded man some time back - when Charles Dance was at the peak of his popularity) 'causes', ballet, opera . . .

So no, I'm not going to come down hard and say 'don't touch that - ever' because climates change and so does popular opinion. And I do firmly believe that, no matter what topic you write about, it's the way you write that Harlequin are looking for. A book with a touchy subject can always be edited, adapted, and I can't believe that they would completely discard anything that was brilliantly written with the emotional power and PTQ they're looking for because it touched on something that wasn't popular. What I will say is that unless you're sure you can do the subject very well and so do it justice, don't risk it as your first submission or as a very very new fledgling writer.

QUESTION:

After a lovemaking scene, will there be changes in the characters' attitudes to each other?

ANSWER

Yes, that's exactly it. There is usually a period of reflection and reconsideration. Sex, especially in a line like Presents/Modern, tends to push the H&h into actions without thinking of consequences and it's only afterwards, in the cold light of day, that reality hits back and makes your characters think 'What have I done!' This is one of the main places where that 'two steps forward and one step back' approach comes into play, so that perhaps the heroine will now back right off, putting up barriers right left and centre.

You would need to show how making love has changed the attitudes of both H&h - either through some internal POV or by some dialogue between them which reveals the changes. Personally, if you can go with the dialogue, then I'd do it. We're back on the 'show don't tell' track here. Even reflection, internal thoughts, are a form of narrative and so can slow the pace of the novel down. Oh, and please, if you put in the H&h's thoughts make them

a. realistic - people's thoughts tend to be broken, chopped up, going one way then another - an ordered, logical and very calculated train of thought reads more like narrative but broken up thoughts become more dramatic, like dialogue.
b. Make them show CHANGES in the person's feelings. I have read too many wouldbes' manuscripts where the heroine expresses the same thoughts over and over and over - wasting

word count, bogging down the development of the plot and quite frankly boring the pants of the reader. If you're going to show a H or h's internal point of view, break it up into small sections and put it in when it SAYS something- shows how things have changed etc.

By the way -seeing as I've mentioned POV here - I should also say that here's another place where there are no hard and fast rules. You can have heroine only POV, dual POV or hero only POV. Write what fits your story and the scene you're writing best.

QUESTION:

Do your characters have to sort out their problems at the same sort of pace? Can one realise how they feel earlier than the other?

ANSWER:

The answer to your question is quite simple - no one ever said that your characters had to have the same amount or the same sort of inner conflict. Really, the very simplest, most basic source of inner conflict in a romance goes like this : She loves him madly. He doesn't love her (or vice versa). That's it. That's really all you need. Obviously, this is such a simple conflict that it's going to be difficult to make it stretch out through a full book - so you add in other bits and pieces to further complicate matters. But what you've raised is in fact an important point. The end of a romance, obviously, has to see all conflict resolved and all the issues arising from it cleared up, sorted out, and tidied away. This is known in the trade as the 'But you said . . .' section. Where all the explanations are brought out, all the difficulties smoothed over , ready for that HEA.

But if you put all of this sorting out into one chapter right at the end it would be very heavy - and pretty boring. The reader would have to plough through explanation after explanation and there would be very little action of any sort. I think most readers would probably skip the last section altogether. So what you do is, exactly what you suggest. You get rid of some of the problems as you go along, clearing some space in the confusion and upset, and then in the last section you clear up the final, and possibly the most difficult thing that has been keeping them apart.

Let me try and give you an example - Rafael's Love-Child:

The causes of conflict are:
1. The heroine (Serena) doesn't know who Rafael is or what part he might have played in her past.
2. Serena doesn't know what happened in her past to put her in hospital
3. Rafael doesn't trust Serena because of what he has been told about her which has made her out to be a liar and a grasping person who would do anything for money.
4. Rafael hates the fact that he is falling madly in love with such a person
5. Serena is falling in love with Rafael but doesn't know if she can trust him. So she doubts her love for him.

Rafael takes her to his house and asks her to help him look after the baby. Watching her with the little boy, he realises she is not the sort of woman he was led to believe. She also comes to trust him and falls even more deeply in love with him. They are moving towards a trust of each other and a passionate relationship. But there is still the problem of what happened in the past. Then when Serena remembers she can explain the lies told about her. But now she doesn't know if she can trust him when he says he loves her because she believes he is only saying this because he wants the baby, not really her.

So some of the original causes of conflict are taken out - the doubts S has about her own love - the doubts R has because of the lies he was told. But some - like the revelation of what happened in the past - and the proof that R loves S for herself are still left to be sorted out. Here, Rafael knows he loves Serena well before the final chapter - but he can't say anything until her conflicts - ie the fact that she doesn't know what happened - are sorted out. But that also means that this other, final conflict of whether he wants her or the baby is created and has to be sorted out too.

QUESTION:

What exactly is 'external conflict'?

ANSWER:

Conflict - external or otherwise - would it make things easier if I called it a 'source of tension' or 'the cause of problems' rather than conflict? I know a lot of people think that when you discuss conflict in a romance you mean that the H&h spend all their time arguing and fighting and being thoroughly unpleasant to each other. But what it really means is that 'conflict' is something - anything - that gets between the H&h and their love and stops them falling into each others' arms and making a lifetime commitment to each other. Without conflict, internal or external, they would meet on the first page, declare their love by the end of the second, get married on the third and live happily ever after. And as the soaps have proved - there is nothing less dramatic than a happy, successful relationship.

So your source of tension is either INTERNAL - that is, it's something in your character's mind that makes them doubt the other's love or hate them for some reason or not trust them. It is the tension that keeps your reader in a state of suspense, wondering if these two will ever see sense and realise that they are perfect for each other if they could only get their act together. In a romance, a lot of the tension must be internal because a romance deals with feelings and it is the tension/conflict between what your H/h WANT and feel - ie to love this person and have him love them - and what they believe- that they can't be trusted/that they only want sex etc etc. This sort of tension arises from the CHARACTER of your H&h and their SITUATION.

Now a situation can be created simply by their internal thoughts - by the lack of trust, the belief that the other has been unfaithful, the thought that one only married the other for money . . . anything that causes a problem. Or the problem can be EXTERNAL - imposed on them from outside by the actions of someone else. In Shakespeare, Romeo & Juliet is a classic example of external conflict/tension. R&J are madly and happily in love - the source of tension between them - the thing that causes a problem and prevents them from getting married and living happily ever after is something outside their relationship and their control - the feud between their families. This sort of conflict could also be where the 'other man' has convinced the heroine that the hero has been unfaithful or where the heroine's mother has intercepted and hidden all the hero's letters so that she thinks he never loved her. In Saturday's Bride, the external conflict is provided by Jenna's family who were opposed to her seeing Connor when she was younger and specifically her older brother who lied to Connor, saying Jenna didn't want to ever see him again, and then to Jenna, saying that Connor hadn't come when she needed him. That's the external bit - the rest of the conflict/tension comes from their feelings of hurt, betrayal, anger etc that result from this and have to be resolved during the book. External conflict is usually easier to clear up than internal because it involved finding a way of showing that the other person/persons were lying and making them reveal the truth, so proving the innocence of the H or h as a result.

So the answer is really as simple as - External conflict (or the source of tension that is not just the H&h's feelings but something outside that) is the problem or one of the problems that keeps the H&h from living happily ever after until they can sort it out. You don't always need an External conflict but you couldn't really have a successful and suspenseful romance without some internal ones.

5. WHY?

When I started this Q&A, I wondered if in fact I should start with WHY? Because I think WHY? is the most important of all. WHY? is the thread that holds the wonderful pearl necklace that is your novel together. Why is the reason everything moves along the path it does and doesn't tie itself up in knots. Why is the little word that gives depths to your characters, logic to your plots, spark to your dialogue and hopefully that little special something that puts the PTQ into your novel and makes it saleable.

Why is WHY? so important? Let me tell you a story.

Some years ago I was in touch with a young and enthusiastic would-be writer. She was a member of this society, had read these books, been to such and such a course and she knew she was going to write for Harlequin (or M&B as this was the UK). So she wanted to give me a synopsis of her story and would I tell her if I thought it was the sort of thing M&B wanted to buy. The synopsis told me that her heroine inherited an island from a distant relative when she got there the Hero was already living on the island. He was furious with h and hated her on sight. Here I interrupted - 'Hang on - WHY?' 'Why what?' 'Why did he hate her on sight?' 'He just did.' 'But why?' 'Well that's what heroes do.'

I drew a long, calming breath. 'But why?'

Some minutes later, when she realised I wasn't going to give in, she grudgingly tossed out,' Well he thought he should have inherited the island himself.' Okay - 'Why?' 'Well, because he wanted   it'   'Why?' I think you'll get the picture. But the rest of her synopsis involved the 'hero' kidnapping the heroine and holding her prisoner on the island ('Because he wanted to') He called her every name under the sun, laughed at her and told her she was shallow and stupid, took all her nice clothes and threw them into the sea (what was that question again? WHY???) He also threw her CD player and all her CDs into the sea, had sex with her (she 'fought against it but very soon gave in'!!!! er - WHY?) then finally she saw a little sense and ran away. But she couldn't stay away from him and she went back to the island to see him (All together now - WHY?) He said he was sorry and he had fallen in love with her from the start and would she marry him - and she said yes.

WHY????

Okay so this is an extreme example. An example of a very bad plot that was based on the belief that HMB heroes 'always' treat their women very badly - for no good reason - and in spite of this the women fall madly in love with their tormentors and marry them.. The hero is abusive, hateful, probably has criminal tendencies, just about rapes the heroine - and then say he loves her and she settles down to marriage with him - the woman must be insane! This one is a bit far fetched but if you add in some major justifications, you might just get the beginnings of a plot out of it. Say - the H had originally been left the island in his grandfather's will but just before his death grandpa had married a much younger second wife who had survived him. She had then bequeathed the island to the h. The H had desperately wanted the island because it was where his mother and father were buried and he had been led to believe that the h intended to turn the place into a tourist village, without a care of anyone else's feelings . You'd still have to work pretty hard to make some of this supposed hero's actions understandable never mind justified, but at least you'd have a start.

As I said earlier, there are only so many plots you can come up with for a romance. It isn't possible to be stunningly original with your story. But if you give your characters convincing reasons WHY they do what they do, WHY they react, WHY they don't trust each other, WHY they come round to trusting eventually, , WHY they fall in love with each other, then you have a hope of getting the dramatic pace, the PTQ, emotional power that an editor is looking for.

And WHY can help you so often when you get stuck. Got 'writer's block'? Look at your last scene and say 'WHY did this happen?' Ask your hero 'WHY did you do that?' or your heroine 'WHY don't you believe him' (and don't take 'I just don't' for an answer.) And the answers should help you move on - because you'll know how they're feeling.

WHY? makes your characters rounded people with depths to them. Asking it gives them inner character as well as the one dimension that appears on the page. WHY? helps you understand their pasts, their hopes, their fears.

WHY? gives you the reason why the 'Black moment' is so very black - for this particular H or h. It explains why something that maybe some other person could shrug off what has happened but he/she can't because . . . (insert your own plot here)

WHY? gives you the reason for a h going to bed with a H - or not - and it gives you the important before and after for any lovemaking. She feels vulnerable WHY? Because she has never heard him say a word of love to her. He feels betrayed. WHY? Because he believes she has only slept with him so that he will help her father . . .(again insert your own reason here)

And WHY gives you the links from one scene to another. The way that scenes link into each other is one of the hardest things for a new writer to grasp. They create a scene, it's wonderfully dramatic, emotional, passionate, sexy, hot - and then the characters move on and the point behind that scene is lost. But if you know WHY something happens - and you should know why everything happens - then you'll know that you'll have to come back to that scene later and link it into what is happening now. As I said before, from the moment your H&h appear on the first page of your story, you should think of them as fully rounded characters. People with pasts, histories, likes, dislikes, fears, hopes, dreams - and you should use those things to explain WHY they are where they are and what they do. Try and think of your book like an elaborate, colourful piece of weaving. When you start out, you have all these strands of wool in a multitude of different colours. It's only when they're all woven together and you see how they make up the pattern - and how that pattern is repeated here - and there - almost the same but subtly different - that you realise how wonderful the whole thing looks. And then it looks as if it could never have been any other way. It's perfect.

You should never create characters who 'just' do something. They should do it *because* - because they can't do anything else. And if you give them strong enough reasons, then even the worst possible behaviour becomes explicable and understandable in the end. And never forget that even in a romance you have to give your H&h reasons to fall in love with one another. We all know that that's what's expected in a romance. That's what inevitably happens, but please make it seem at least likely and not the sort of action that will get your H or h certified as clinically insane.

QUESTION:

I understand how you need to know WHY things happen, but how can you thread this through your plot so that it runs smoothly and doesn't create heavy blocks of backstory?

ANSWER:

Backstory again. It can be tricky - as I said, it's important to weave it in and not put it in lumps. First of all, I think you need to ask yourself some questions. Questions like: Is this part of the backstory really vital to the present day plot? Is this what is affecting my H/h in the present day or just detail that is 'embroidering' the information I need to get across?

Can I get my H /h to tell this to someone (preferably the hero or heroine, depending on who's speaking) so that it is revealed in dialogue in the present romance and not as a major flashback?

Do I really need to give this information in such detail or can I summarise it quickly?

Could I give this information more clearly and dramatically in a chapter that formed the first chapter of the book - or even a prologue - rather than as flashbacks?

Flashbacks always slow down the telling of the present day romance. Use them only where the detail is necessary. If you wonder if some information has been brought in too early, ask yourself - has my reader come to know my characters well enough in the present to care about events that happened in the past and are affecting them now? If your reader doesn't know your character in the present yet, then dropping back into the past too early will confuse and distract them. Always ask yourself 'Is this journey back in time really necessary?' You only have a short word count for most category romance novels. Ask yourself whether the words you want to spend in the past could be put to better, more dramatic, more emotional use in the present. Because the present story always affects the reader much more than the past.

6. HOW

You didn't think I'd forget HOW did you?

Well - I'll be honest - I can't teach you how. HOW is what you bring to this. I've given you what I can - the WHO WHERE WHEN WHAT and of course that WHY that you need to think about putting into your book. HOW you put them all together is up to you. It's the way you do it that will give it that touch of something special (I hope) that will make it all yours and yours alone.

We all know what the plot of a romance is - as I said in the introduction to this Q&A Hero meets heroine, they fall in love, there are problems and difficulties in the way of that love, those problems are resolved - they live happily ever after. But if I can steal the perfect quote from a wonderful writer Michelle Reid - we all know about the happy ending - it's how you get there that is the story. And how you and your characters get there is the book that you write.

12

Kate's 12 Point Plan for Writing Category Romance:

(This is a transcript of an internet chat I did on writing romance with a group of writers)

The 12 Points:

1. Emotion emotion emotion

2 Conflict

3 Dialogue

4. Sharp focus on Hero and heroine - no sub plots

5. Sensuality

6. Passion

7. Sophisticated hero

8. Sympathetic heroine

9. Vital vulnerability

10 The question WHY?

11.Intense black moment

12.Believable Happy ever after

KW = Kate Walker
C = One of the chat group

KW: So - 1. Emotion: 'Emotion, emotion, emotion' - That's a direct quote from an editor – what sells is Emotion emotion emotion. Or, as the great Emma Darcy once said - think of the emotion you think you need in a story - and then double it!

C: My first try was rejected because of lack of emotional punch and excitement.

KW: That's SO common - almost all the first tries get that! Many new submissions to Harlequin receive the common criticisms that it lacks the 'emotional punch' or 'emotional velocity' that makes a published novel and fails to achieve a satisfactory emotional climax. These are terms that writers often have difficulty understanding. 'Emotional velocity' is the impact that a story has on the reader. Over the course of the story, the characters' troubles should grow worse, larger, harder to handle, seemingly more insoluble. The characters' emotional involvement - and hence the reader's involvement with the characters - grows right along with the difficulties the characters face. This means that the 'line' of the novel which should move in zigzags, like the letter W - going up through tension to a painful pitch, then coming down to a more peaceful stage, only to shoot upwards again as something new is added. There should be some form of resolution along the way - some improvement in circumstances that then is destroyed by a further development - two steps forward, one step back.

KW: Which brings me to point 2 - the reason for the emotion – is Conflict - But conflict is not just arguing and sniping and being nasty. You need to have a conflict that really matters. Something that the hero and heroine really really care about and so it will really hurt if it keeps going and isn't resolved finally.

C: Life and death stuff?

KW: Life and death - emotional life and death – heartbreaking stuff - family splitting up stuff – Make it something that it's worth being in conflict about. And don't forget that there is INTERNAL conflict – where the problems come from inside the hero and/or heroine's head – and EXTERNAL conflict where the problem is something imposed from outside – like Romeo and Juliet where their families are feuding. Yes?

C: Yes.

KW: Number 3 - Dialogue. A book should try to be at least 60% dialogue no more than 40% narrative. The old 'show don't tell'. And dialogue brings it alive, makes it immediate - gives the conflict and the emotion

C: Kate, how much dialogue is too much?

KW: Really, you can never have too much. Not unless you have the whole book in dialogue!

C: Thanks

KW: You need some narrative- scene setting - actions etc but dialogue is good. Okay 4 - sharp FOCUS on your hero and heroine. Secondary characters dilute the tension and so dilute the   emotion.

C: So keep hero and heroine centre stage all the time?

KW: Yes - that's what the reader wants she wants to see - the hero and heroine and their conflict. If you have to have them separated, then try to make it for as short a time as possible. You don't want the reader to lose sight of hero, even if the heroine does. The same goes for secondary characters - You might need a spare character or two - the heroine's boyfriend or her mother, or the hero's brother or something but use them as little as possible

C: Which is why isolation storylines – like being trapped in a cottage by the snow or something similar - work so well?

KW: Yes - get your hero and heroine somewhere where they can't be interrupted no matter what happens and you can be on to a winner. This is especially important for the shorter Harlequin Mills and Boon lines - for the 55,000 word book where a tight focus matters.

KW: 5 Sensuality

KW: says: There's a belief that some of the category lines allow no sexual content – but this is one of those ancient myths, best forgotten. Different lines have different approaches. For example, the USA Romance line (Tender in UK and Sweet in Australia) is probably the most restrained in this .For Presents (Modern/Sexy) it's a different story – there's plenty of passion and sensuality.

That doesn't just mean a sex scene though. More importantly, it's the build up to something - the gathering storm – the anticipation - the PTQ. PTQ anyone? Know what that is?

C: page turning quality

KW: Yes. Page Turning Quality. The build up of tension and excitement that keeps the reader turning page after page. There is more tension in anticipation than in the actual fulfilment. So if you put in a sex scene too early or too fast it comes a bit too soon.

C: Is there any rule when you should actually have a love scene?

KW: No rules. You let your characters decide

C: Gottcha - thanks.

KW: says, I have one book where the love scene is in Chapter 2 - I think - and that was very passionate - and another where nothing happened till the penultimate chapter - but the tension built up all the way through

C: How do you do that?

KW: You need to build the sensual atmosphere all along - with touches, glances, smiles, scents, clothes etc. You use all the senses to communicate that. Which means that by the time you get your build up completed - it's like the countdown to a rocket launch- 10, 9, 8 7- blast off!
   KW: says, All of which brings us to 6 - which is passion. Now passion is not just sex - it's intensity. It's that conflict and emotion and tension and all the rest of it. So if they're deeply involved in whatever -whether arguing, joking, eating - loving - it's intense and heightened. Think of how you feel when you're so deeply involved that everything is sharp and so clear it's almost painful. That's the sort of sensitivity of the heroine and hero to each other that you're aiming for.

C: 7 is the hero
KW: says, Okay - Hero – In a Presents/Modern novel he's usually sophisticated, probably alpha male. Rich, powerful, successful, gorgeous etc etc. Again, though, there is plenty of scope in other lines for a more beta hero – more the boy next door.
C: Ok

KW: says, But the important thing is to create the sort of man who, even if you stripped all that away, could still be amazing, stunning, devastating and first class husband material. The trappings are just that - trappings - props - easy ways to show he's alpha - but you should be able to imagine that without them he'd still be stunning.

C: Does the relationship have to end in marriage?

KW: In a category novel - commitment - which these days usually means marriage or the promise of it.

C: OK. Thanks.

KW: lot of editors want you to show the wedding. But there are lines where that conventional ending can be turned on its head. Category romance still usually ends on the happy ever after note.

C: So we have the Alpha hero -

KW: and then we have the heroine who must be sympathetic to the reader.

That's sympathetic – not pathetic!

C: Not the sweet innocent virgin that everyone imagines then?

KW: She can be innocent and sweet if you want her to. But no whimpering wimps, no doormats, no simpering sillies. A modern young women.

C: Believable, realistic heroines?

KW: That's right. But the sympathy bit fits with the hero as well - which is why the dual point of view (POV) is now so popular. This way, the hero can behave very badly indeed (actually the heroine can as well) as long as the reader knows why. What the reader doesn't want is a hero - or a heroine - that they can't understand. They want to know why they're behaving in this way, even if they are doing something the reader wouldn't like. For example – in The Hostage Bride - the hero kidnaps the heroine - on the surface, not a good thing. But the reader has some idea of why he's done it so she'll go along and bear with his behaviour

C: Because it's for an endearing reason.

KW: And we get an insight into how his feelings change along the way. Now where were we? Ah yes – sympathy. So you can let your characters do a lot of things that might seem not appropriate to a hero or a heroine so long as they have good reasons that seem to them to justify it at the time – not just bad temper or whatever.
C: Why especially the heroine?

KW: You specially don't want to lose reader identification with your heroine because she is the reader's eyes. The reader tends to see all action – and the hero through her and you want the reader to understand and sympathise with her. And this brings us to point 9 – vital vulnerability. This is the chink in the armour, the reason why they're doing something - the soft heart inside the armour that the hero has surrounded himself with because of something in his past. Or the reason why the hero says he wants a marriage of convenience and if she marries him he'll pay all her debts – and her reasons for accepting. So you can see that if you get the sympathy for the hero, you also get a way for the heroine to reach him and touch him, no matter how tough and cynical he may seem

C: It all goes back to character motivation?

KW: Yes character motivation romances are not really plot-driven
at all but CHARACTER driven

KW: says, Which brings me to my favourite point, the one I'm always saying is the most important - the 10th point is The Question WHY

Why does he/she do this why does he feel this way/ why does she react this way etc Any time you're stuck you should look at your character and ask why are they in this position/mood whatever. Why did they say whatever they said that got them there.
 Too many people move their characters around as if they were cardboard cut-outs in a toy theatre when the characters should move themselves. That clear?

 C: Perfectly.

KW: Great. Just two points left: 11 - that black moment In some lines, such as Presents/Modern it needs to be BLACK - we're back at intensity and conflict again. If the conflict has been intense and passionate then the worst moment should seem impossible to mend - not just something that could be dealt with a 'But what I meant was . . . '

C: Oh I hate that in books - when they just need to explain
KW: So do I. What I like to do is a sort of double ending - the double climax. So just when things are looking as if they are starting to go right and it's all going well and they're about to fall into each others' arms - you introduce another spanner in the works. Something that you've laid a clue to at the

beginning of the book and now you bring in like the wicked witch in a pantomime to make things go wrong again

C: Hang on, I think I get it. You bring them to an almost-happy-ending then interrupt it with a Black Moment - then get the real happy ending, right?

KW: That's just it. Okay point 12 - is the Happy ending - but it has to be a BELIEVABLE happy ending. No simple, easy, sorry love but I was in a bad mood sort of explanations, no instant falling into his arms and forgiving and forgetting instantly

What I mean is that if the hero's been an arrogant swine all the way through he's going to have to keep some of that pride even when he crumbles

If the heroine has been provoking him all the way through, she's going to provoke him at the end too.

If there are other people involved - people whose lies say have helped create the conflict then their part needs to be resolved and the hero and heroine's reactions to them need to be sorted out.

C: I have to profess a dislike of the unequal ending

KW: Unequal ending - can you give a for example?

C: Where the heroine or hero gives up something special, and the other makes no compromise

KW: I agree - both should meet the other halfway, A modern relationship - and a romance is really a relationship novel - usually works on some sort of compromise So your characters need to work out the compromise they can live with - there should be no winner, no loser just equals.

KW: So that's the points covered – any questions?

C: How do Beta men differ from Alphas and how do they fit into romance?

KW: Alpha men - I said the Presents/Modern hero is an alpha - rich, sexy, powerful, successful etc but I also said that he should be strong enough to lose all the trappings of riches etc and still be strong. A Beta man is more like the 'New Man' and man who is kind, gentle, looks after babies, cook's that sort of thing. You'll find him in the other lines – such as Romance (Tender Romance in the UK). There's room for both in romance.

C: I thought Beta's were *sweet* heroes?

KW: Yes, Beta are sweet 'Tender'; heroes - but what you get the best of both worlds with is if you have an Alpha male admitting he has the Beta in him as well - for the love of this woman who has enthralled him. If you do it right you can have an Alpha male who can still do all those things - he can be a Beta inside

C: why is the alpha so important?

KW: The alpha is the purest form of fantasy - the Real Man who thinks he doesn't need love – but really he does. He's the sort of hero that Heathcliff or Mr Rochester was in the Bronte novels – a man who feels intensely but doesn't have the emotional vocabulary to express it

C: Lately romances seem to be going back to younger heroines Like 21-22. Is that coincidence or a trend?

KW: Some readers – and some writers prefer to have a virginal heroine. That's one of the reasons for a younger heroine. You can't have a very believable virgin these days if she's much older. You have to have good reasons for it.

C: So are virginal heroines a requirement of a category romance?

KW: Answer - no - or yes - depending on your plot. What I mean is it's totally up to you. You can have a virgin, someone who's been married, widowed, divorced, had a live-in lover. Like I said, these are modern young women – unless of course you're writing a Historical romance.

C: Women over 30?

KW: Again depends on plot

C: And children?

KW: Yes- same goes - she can have children - so can he. You write the story with the hero and heroine you want and need for the plot you have planned.

C: Kate, you mentioned not having a lot of secondary characters...

KW: yes

C: can you use them to play a pivotal role in getting the heroine and hero together? What about using them as a foil to show up hero/heroine's weaknesses and strengths. For eg. Tough hero - beta chum.

KW: You can have a secondary character /s who play roles in bringing hero and heroine together and as a foil, yes. For example, one of my heroes had a gay guy as a friend. But remember that focus on the hero and heroine. In a shorter book, you don't want other characters to dilute it - and you will find you have a better ending if the hero and heroine come to the resolution themselves

C: Question about kids...all the ones I've read, the other parent is out of the picture, is having the ex around taboo?

KW: Ex can be around – but with an ex-wife, for example - it's a cliché to make her a real bitch. Makes the hero look a fool for ever having married her. A rounded character is more interesting

C: Actually, I was thinking more in terms of heroine's ex...visiting the kids and such, having to balance that with new romance,   etc.

KW: Yes - that's a modern dilemma and one that can well be woven in. The heroine would have torn loyalties yes?

C: Absolutely

KW: And it would be an important conflict -one that would mean   a
lot to both of them

C: Course, messy stuff...the best way to make it

KW: Yes, messy - and needing work and love and understanding and compromise to work it out. And conflict along the way

KW: Okay, I have to round this off now – so I'll give you some basic information – advice on how to prepare yourself to write - the things an editor is likely to be looking for. These are the sort of things that I find are frequently the problem with beginners at writing, especially for category romance.

It is a specialised field, which demands particular things from its authors and the best way possible to learn what those are is to read, read, read. Read as many novels as you can and try to see where the different authors are close to being the same and where they differ - because no two authors ever write exactly the same, no matter how close they may seem. That's the best place to start.

Your novel should show above all else that you have read some of the current output by the publisher you are aiming at. It should have lively dialogue, show awareness of the fact that characters need to have pasts and histories as well as appearing on the page from the first chapter, and you should make your characters sympathetic and interesting.

It's important not to fall into the all too common trap of trying to make your hero totally ruthless and callous, only changing as he declares his love at the very end. There should be a flow of mood, between attraction and dislike, anger and affection. And above all you need to show the characters' developing feelings through their thoughts and words. This shows an understanding of the format of a romance which is very good starting point

If you were to submit a novel to an editor, in the hope of publication, what she would be looking for would be:

Lively characters, with an individual twist to them.

A 'pace' to the novel that keeps it moving swiftly from one scene to the next, not slowing and losing the reader at any time.

An emotional drive that would give the story that essential PTQ (page turning quality) which means the reader cares for the characters and wants them to 'live happily ever after'.

An individual 'voice' that meant the author was telling the story in her own way and not just as a copy of everything that has gone before.

The story should obviously be well written, have a beginning, middle and an end, characters who are more than just one-dimensional cardboard cut-outs, but be careful that it doesn't just read more like a pale copy of so much that has gone before rather than a story that you desperately wanted to write about characters with whom you were involved and who you cared about. I would suggest that you could improve your chances immensely by becoming deeply involved with your hero and heroine, getting to know them as well as you possibly can, and letting the plot come from them, rather than trying to think of a traditional romance plot. Lose yourself in their story, write from the heart, and give the novel an emotional edge by making it clear that your hero and heroine have a great deal to lose if their relationship fails. All this will add to the emotional punch of your writing. The deeper the conflict, the more emotional commitment the characters will make to it. They need to be in conflict about something worth fighting over, not just a simple disagreement of a misunderstanding that can be solved by a few questions or a reasonable discussion.

It's important that the things they do together have variety. We should see a different side of each of them when they appear throughout the book
. There should be surprises, emotional shocks, changes of heart all the way through not just at the very end. The sexual attraction should also be fierce and potent. There is no need to have many intensely detailed, physical lovemaking scenes in a romance, but there should always be a great deal of sexual tension, the 'fizz' of excitement between your two characters.

But the emotional tension is vital. The reader wants to become deeply involved with your characters, to really care for them, and to feel that they are risking real pain, real loss, real heartache in the relationship they are involved in. You need to involve yourself more with your characters, up the emotional stakes, and lose yourself in their story.

Point of view - My advice is to use what works for you and what works for your story. Some of my books have no hero's POV in them. But many - most - of my latest books have plenty of what's going on inside the hero's head. You have to do what works for you and your story. But if you are going to put in your hero's thoughts, make them read like masculine thoughts – not just something almost identical to the heroine's opinions. Finally, is it difficult for a new author to get read? Yes and no. The 'slush pile' is looked at by the editors regularly - they ask for a synopsis and three chapters to look at. I've been told by USA writers and Canadians that Presents/Modern is only open to new English authors. Many English would-be writers have said the exact opposite to me - that they think Presents/Modern Romance for example is closed to all but new American authors! The truth is that editors are actively looking for new talent. But many more people think they can write for Harlequin Mills & Boon than actually can! I'm afraid the submission rate is high and the acceptance rate is very low. But the doors are not closed. No editor is going to turn down a well-written, emotionally appealing story with interesting characters and an individual voice! They would love to sign more people to write for them - if only they could find them!

13

ON TARGETING

Many 'how to' books talk about targeting a particular publisher or a specific line within that publisher's output – Harlequin Mills & Boon and Silhouette are particularly relevant here. But I've often been asked, 'Won't this destroy my originality?' 'Wouldn't it be better just to write the book of my heart and then find a publisher for it?'

Well, yes. This is one approach. But the world of publishing – and particularly that of publishing romance – is so competitive and crowded these days, that a little forward planning can hopefully speed up the process and increase your chances of success.

It's precisely because the differences between some lines can seem so slight that you need to consider exactly which line you're writing for when you are working - or the book of your heart (which might very well be a perfectly fine book) can end up being severely messed about - and not to its good.

Look at it this way. If you simply set out to write the book of your heart, without even at least having thought about which line you're aiming for you can waste an awful amount of time. Say you write the book and send it to line A Editor A thinks it has too many sensual scenes for her line - she sends it back to you

If you're really lucky - and believe me, it's rare- she'll:

(1) tell you why she sent it back.
More likely it will be
(2) Just sent with a form letter - these are the usual reasons why we return mss.

If it's (1) You could get to work on it, cut all the sensual scenes, and then find that she still rejects it. And you might have cut the heart out of your book because the book of your heart might be a Presents/Modern or a Blaze

If it's (2) Then you could send it to another line - having no idea really why it came back - and so not knowing which one to try for the best - and you could be trying and trying again for years - because we all know how long it can take an editor to get to read a book!

Okay, so targeting will save you time at the submitting stage. It will also save you time and energy at the writing stage.

Say you happily write your novel putting in plenty of mystery, intrigue, lots of secondary characters, some highly passionate scenes. Then you think about where to submit it - and you'll find that you'll come up against a 'pruning' problem. Send it to one line and they could say :

"Good book - but you need to cut the secondary characters.'
OR
'Good book but you need to cut out the intrigue'
OR
'Good book but you need to cut the sex'

And that's only if they bother to say anything!

So now you are faced with the fact that you have to cut X thousand of your precious words - which is hard enough. It's like a cutting off part of your baby! But equally you have to think of something else to put in its place. Which can be even harder.

And all the while, time is passing. You're editing the book again - and if you're not careful you can edit the life out of it. The more times you rework a novel, the less of the spontaneous, passionate, from the heart stuff you leave in. And what started off as something with a heart and soul and guts can end up as a pale shadow of itself. And I should know I've been there. I once rewrote a book five times - each time according to what an editor wanted - and killed it stone dead.

But all this can be avoided if you do a little thinking beforehand. I'm not saying that you should work on your novel with the demands of the line and nothing else in mind. Nor am I saying that you should focus so intently and twist it and torture it into a shape it wasn't meant to have in the first place - but I am saying that you should know whether you're aiming at a line that has secondary characters and subplots, or focuses fiercely on the main romance. Or one that has mystery and intrigue - or not. Or one that has strongly passionate scenes and fairly explicit ones or prefers to have a more gentle, restrained approach. Because if you don't you could waste a lot of precious writing time writing scenes/characters that could just end up filed in the recycle bin.

This is part one! The other questions - like when is a book a Blaze and when is it an Intrigue - is a different matter.

As a writer for Presents/Modern I frequently come across writers - even published writers - who tell me that the 'difference' between Presents/Modern and Romance Tender is just one thing - SEX.

Romance has no sex in it. Presents have lots.

Right?

WRONG!

If it was that simple, it would also be an easy matter to write a Romance/Tender book and then turn it into a Presents/Modern simply by adding a couple of steamy bedroom scenes. But that isn't the case. And as many authors and would-be authors have found, there are plenty of

Romances out there with lots of sensuality and - scenes where the H&h 'do it' in the course of the story

If you're looking at the difference between Presents/Modern and Romance/Tender, I always feel that it can be a mistake to concentrate just on the sexual aspect of the books. Yes, there is usually more physical passion and activity in a Presents/Modern than in a Romance/Tender , but you need to consider the other aspects too.

I think it comes back to that word intensity - and putting that together with emotion. In a Presents/Modern the emotions and the passions are intense and fierce - they are books that always balance precariously on the borderline between happiness and tragedy because the central characters have such potential to hurt each other. It's those Alpha heroes fighting against their own feelings as well as everything else! But it's those strong emotions, the deep issues between the H&h, the intense clashes that make a Presents/Modern novel.

Tender Romances tend to be warmer, gentler, but still full of emotion, more 'plot based'

So when you're looking at a line, not just from the point of view of reading and enjoying it, but with the idea of writing for it you need to consider so many things. You're looking at:

EMPHASIS - how much is given to which aspects of the story. So with the question of whether a book is a Blaze or an Intrigue, it's whether the emphasis is on the sexual relationship (Blaze) or solving the mystery (Intrigue)

INTENSITY - an example would be Presents/Modern versus Romance/Tender . In a Tender Romance it's perfectly possible to have your H&h actually like each other all the way through - in a presents that would be rare. Though Michelle Reid writes wonderful books where the H&h are so obviously in love all the way through - and even admit it - but they still tear each other to pieces because of other circumstances.

CHARACTERS - in a Presents too many other characters would diffuse the intensity. In a Super romance more characters would be an asset.

SEX - yes, this has to be considered, but as I said it's not that in one line it's not allowed and in another it is - you can have a book where there is just one major passionate scene but it is a Presents/Modern because of the - that word again - intensity - of the rest of the relationship. Or one where they make love openly and clearly on the page but because the atmosphere is very different it is a gentler Tender Romance.

CONFLICT - this is a major point in deciding which line you're aiming for. Obviously, from what I've been saying, a line like Presents/Modern has greater scope for a stronger conflict (But make sure you don't confuse 'conflict' with simply 'argument') And in an Intrigue then the conflict needs to be based around the mystery element.

SUBPLOTS - does the line have room and word count enough for them or not - once again it's the emphasis that makes the difference.

And once you've considered these for the lines, you need to consider them for your own work - and of course your own reading. Which do you prefer? Why?

I started writing before there was a split between Romance/Tender and Presents/Modern here in the UK - but if there had been that split, I know which line I would have wanted to read most - which one I would have enjoyed most. And so if I'd known there had to be a choice - and there has to be a choice because you have to send your ms to a particular editor on a particular line - I know I'd have chosen Presents/Modern and I'd have slanted my ms that way. I've written both in my time and I know that the differences between them can be subtle and perhaps difficult to see - but they are there. Ask anyone who loves a particular line and they'll tell you.

That way you can still write the book of your heart, but if
you put something in - or leave something out - you'll have a
better idea of which line editor is likely to be most interested in
it.

www.straightforwardco.co.uk

All titles, listed below, in the Straightforward Guides Series can be purchased online, using credit card or other forms of payment by going to www.straightfowardco.co.uk A discount of 25% per title is offered with online purchases.

Law
A Straightforward Guide to:
Consumer Rights
Bankruptcy Insolvency and the Law
Employment Law
Private Tenants Rights
Family law
Small Claims in the County Court
Contract law
Intellectual Property and the law
Divorce and the law
Leaseholders Rights
The Process of Conveyancing
Knowing Your Rights and Using the Courts
Producing Your own Will
Housing Rights
The Bailiff the law and You
Probate and The Law
Company law
What to Expect When You Go to Court
Guide to Competition Law
Give me Your Money-Guide to Effective Debt Collection
Caring for a Disabled Child

General titles
Letting Property for Profit
Buying, Selling and Renting property
Buying a Home in England and France
Bookkeeping and Accounts for Small Business

Creative Writing
Freelance Writing
Writing Your own Life Story
Writing performance Poetry
Writing Romantic Fiction
Speech Writing

Teaching Your Child to Read and write
Teaching Your Child to Swim
Raising a Child-The Early Years

Creating a Successful Commercial Website
The Straightforward Business Plan
The Straightforward C.V.
Successful Public Speaking

Handling Bereavement
Play the Game-A Compendium of Rules
Individual and Personal Finance
Understanding Mental Illness
The Two Minute Message
Guide to Self Defence
Buying a Used Car
Tiling for Beginners

Go to:

www.straightforwardco.co.uk

Freelance Writing
Writing Your own Life Story
Writing performance poetry
Writing Romantic Fiction
Speech Writing

Understanding Mental Illness